D1238050

Vintage Home

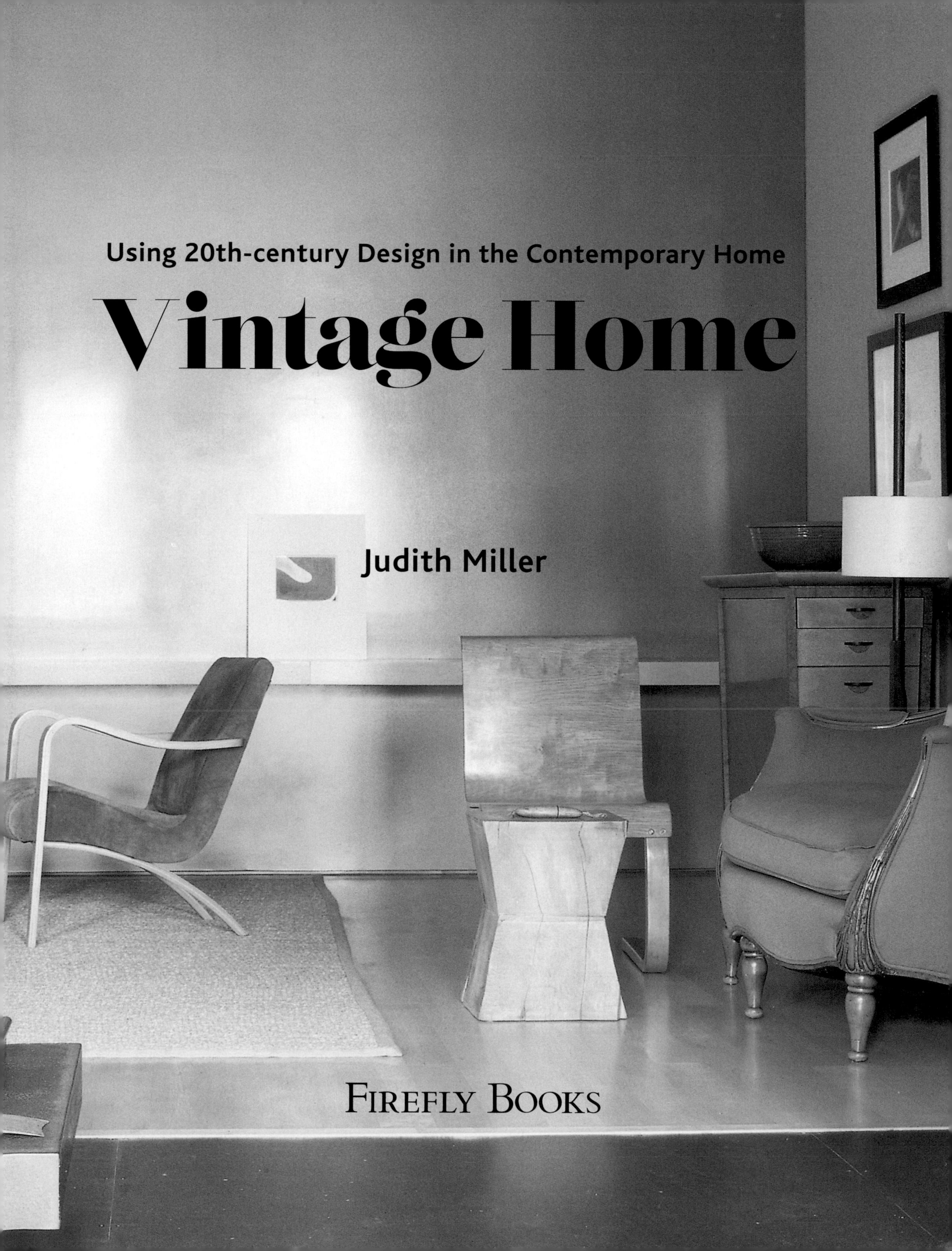

Using 20th-century Design in the Contemporary Home

Vintage Home

Judith Miller

FIREFLY BOOKS

A FIREFLY BOOK

Published by Firefly Books Ltd. 2015

Text copyright © 2015 by Judith Miller
Design and layout copyright © 2015
Jacqui Small

All rights reserved. No part of this
publication may be reproduced, stored
in a retrieval system, or transmitted in
any form or by any means, electronic,
mechanical, photocopying, recording
or otherwise, without the prior written
permission of the Publisher.

First printing

**Publisher Cataloging-in-Publication
Data (U.S.)**

Miller, Judith, 1951–
   Vintage homes : using 20th-century
design in the contemporary home /
Judith Miller.
[288] pages : color illustrations ; cm.
Includes index.
Summary: "This is a collector's guide to
and a celebration of furniture, lighting
and decorative objects from Art Deco
to the space age. From serious and
costly designer creations to cheerful
mass-produced kitsch, this title looks
at objects from around the world that
were made for every taste and budget."
— from Publisher.

ISBN-13: 978-1-77085-612-7
   1. Interior decoration. 2. Antiques
in interior decoration. 3. Collectibles in
interior decoration. I. Title.
747 dc23   NK2110.M455 2014

**Library and Archives Canada
Cataloguing in Publication**

Miller, Judith, 1951–, author
   Vintage home : using 20th-century
design in the contemporary home /
Judith Miller.
Includes index.
ISBN 978-1-77085-612-7 (bound)
   1. Interior decoration. 2. Antiques
in interior decoration. 3. Collectibles in
interior decoration. I. Title.
NK2110.M56 2015   747
C2015-900452-7

Published in the United States by
Firefly Books (U.S.) Inc.
P.O. Box 1338, Ellicott Station
Buffalo, New York 14205

Published in Canada by
Firefly Books Ltd.
50 Staples Avenue, Unit 1
Richmond Hill, Ontario L4B 0A7

Printed in China

Valuations

The stars included in captions indicate the
following price ranges:

Under $1,500	★ ★ ★ ★ ★
$1,500–$15,499	★ ★ ★ ★ ★
$15,500–$39,999	★ ★ ★ ★ ★
$40,000–$79,999	★ ★ ★ ★ ★
$80,000–$149,999	★ ★ ★ ★ ★
£150,000+	★ ★ ★ ★ ★ ★

NPA: no price available

First published in 2015 by
Jacqui Small LLP
74–77 White Lion Street
London N1 9PF

Publisher: Jacqui Small
Senior Commissioning Editor: Eszter Karpati
Managing Editor: Emma Heyworth-Dunn
Senior Designer: Rachel Cross
Editor: Sian Parkhouse
Production: Maeve Healy

Contents

What is Vintage?

In recent years the term "vintage" has come to mean so much more than something old and well made that is not yet an antique. It can be used loosely to describe something just a few years old but still desirable (these pieces are sometimes called "retro") as well as something that is decades old and close to antique status.

Its appeal has grown as buyers have turned away from homogenized, disposable, flatpack furniture and mass-produced home accessories and come to see the value in reusing and recycling beautiful objects from the past. Many are returning to the styles their parents and grandparents enjoyed with a new appreciation, and giving these pieces a new lease on life. For the purpose of this book, the term "vintage" covers the many decorative styles of the 20th century. Whether they are classed as Art Deco, Mid-Century Modern, or Minimalist, these pieces are the antidote to "brown" furniture—the standard polished-wood, Georgian and Victorian designs that furnished many homes for decades. Their creators were considered to be modern in their day, and many of these pieces still appear strikingly modern, despite their age.

Vintage furnishings are old and have a fascinating history, but they may not be classed as antiques—although their price tags may suggest that they are. Many examples were made by famous designers whose work is celebrated in museums, but others may be one-off, beautiful designs created by an unknown hand but cherished through the years. Serious buyers avoid new pieces designed to look old and created to satisfy the demand for the vintage look.

One of the beauties of vintage interiors is that while purists will keep to a particular style, others feel free to mix pieces from different design eras to create an original and eclectic look. This also means that they can make a feature of special pieces by giving them a backdrop of complementary objects that are not necessarily in the same style or from the same era.

Another benefit is that vintage pieces can be found everywhere, from discerning stores whose buyers source and sell items from around the world, to antique shops full of potential treasures, and yard sales and thrift sales where those with an eye for style can make their own design discoveries.

Once you have found the vintage look you like, be sure to keep looking for it—you will spot examples everywhere that will enhance your rooms.

Homages to 20th-century design abound in this contemporary interior (*opposite*). In front of a scrap-metal screen by **Hunziker** and **David Gulassa**, which recalls in its configuration the blocks of color of a Piet Mondrian painting, stand an **Alvar Aalto**-style cantilevered chair, a Deco lampstand, a Classical-Deco sofa, and a Post Modern wood-block table.

Mixing eras

The design movements that developed during the 20th century show a breadth of influences and styles that reflect the social and political changes of their times. As international communication became faster, ideas and possibilities were shared and helped to inspire new ideas and forms. Magazines, exhibitions, and trade fairs brought the work of designers to a wide and appreciative public. World wars, international financial boom and recession, and concern over the environment meant that many themes and inspirations became universal rather than parochial.
All design is new and modern in its own time, but before the 19th century when designers such as Christopher Dresser

Vinyl-upholstered, Art Deco-style slipper chairs are successfully combined with 1960s icons—**Eero Aarnio**'s acrylic Bubble chair and **Achille Castiglioni**'s aluminum Arco lamp—in this large, contemporary living space (*right*).

Launched in Britain in 1953 by E. Gomme, and advertised by the J. Walter Thompson agency, the G Plan range made post-war "modern" furniture design financially viable for many ordinary homeowners (*below*).

and Josef Hoffman began to show their work, most "new" designs looked to the past for inspiration, whether it was ancient Rome or medieval Europe. The late 19th century saw a new breed of radical designers looking to the future for their inspiration, and this continued in the 20th century as society began to reject the past.

By and large the results were revolutionary. Cantilevered chairs, glass-topped tables, sofas made of nothing but wire all challenged the status quo and brought about hundreds of imitators. Where designers did look to the past—whether it was French Art Deco furniture designers or 1950s Italian glassmakers—they turned the motifs and styles they found there and took them to the extreme, making them almost unrecognizable. And while a pure, streamlined Art Deco or Post Modern interior may provide a showcase for the designs of a particular period or group of designers, the breadth of styles and materials used during the 20th century means that it is possible—some might say beneficial—to combine elements from many styles to create one of your own.

The simplest way to incorporate a piece of vintage style into a room is to make it the focal point. Many vintage styles were designed to be used in rooms decorated with the minimum of fuss: walls covered with plain or minimal patterns, large windows to let in plenty of natural light, pale and neutral drapes or shades, and plain or wooden floor coverings allow the furnishings to speak for themselves. Set an Eames chair, Tom Dixon lamp, or Le Corbusier daybed against a plain, neutral wall and you have a piece of functional furniture that also makes a statement and becomes the focal point of the room.

There are no rules with this style of vintage interior so feel free to mix and match designers and eras to create a set of diverse dining-room chairs or use the same color of upholstery to mix and match armchairs and sofas. Then use individual elements such as colored cushions and rugs and eye-catching artworks to bring the look together through color and texture.

However, as many vintage styles use the same materials or color palette, it is easy to combine them for an eclectic result. For example, Bauhaus, Art Deco, and Mid-Century Modern designers all used chrome-plated metal frames for chairs and tables, while Modernist and Mid-Century Modern furniture was made from bent plywood, and Mid-Century Modern and Post Modern chairs feature bold blocks of color.

Displaying a collection of ceramics or glass that complement one another is another way to bring a splash of vintage style to a room. Make a virtue of the fact that Czech and Murano glass from the 1950s and '60s are often confused by combining pieces on a shelf or within a cabinet. Perhaps you could theme the glass by color or style—maybe try an array of ashtrays or bowls in different sizes. Similarly, Art Deco ceramics and 1950s Art pottery often feature stylized figures. Ceramicists from both eras favored the female form as a decorative element, and a collection of these objects will transform a corner or credenza. Alternatively, use these makers' fascination with animals or mythical beings to create a decorative thread.

Other themes that were repeated during the 20th century include advances in science and the space race. Use atom- and outer space-themed lamps, posters, and clocks to bring this concept to life. Travel also became faster and more affordable with developments in the motor industry, the possibility of air travel and package holidays. Celebrate this with travel posters and streamlined accessories.

Use the graphic shapes common to many vintage pieces to create sculptural landscapes within a room setting. The metal elements of a Charles and Ray Eames chair, Warren Platner wire table, and Gino Sarfatti lamp will bring a geometric feel to a dining room.

Alternatively, allow the architecture of a room to guide you as you select the pieces to furnish it. For example, a living room with a low fireplace might benefit from low benches and coffee tables that allow the sitters to be at the same level as the flames. The result will be fresh, new, and yet unashamedly vintage.

In the dining area of a 1960s Long Island cottage, transformed by architect Annabelle Selldorf, stylistically eclectic furnishings, albeit mostly from the 1950s and '60s, are pulled harmoniously together by the subtle use of graduated color (*opposite*). The pale yellow of the **Fornasetti** chairs is echoed in the map, and then strengthened to yellow ocher in one of the '50s sideboard's sliding doors. This morphs into the mid-tan of the leather-upholstered side chairs, also picked up in the darker tones of the Berber rug. All are, in turn, grounded by the dark brown of the wooden floor, dining table, sliding sideboard door, and the light frame above—the shades of the last providing, together with two bowls and the plant form, a complementary green accent.

While steel-footed and -framed sofas, chairs, and tables make a substantial contribution to it, as does a striped rug, and while the organic contrast of a large cactus serves to highlight it, the clarity of the rectilinear design of this loft-space living room (*above*) is most firmly established by the large, white modular storage and display unit designed by **George Nelson**.

Stand-out fixtures and fittings include a glass-and-steel tension bridge, and an open walnut staircase inspired by Japanese tansu chests (*opposite*). Furnishing equivalents include a wooden **Charles** and **Ray Eames** LCW chair and a blue **Eero Saarinen** Womb chair.

The Birth of Modernism

1880–1914

The historical eclecticism of the second half of the
19th century gave way to a concern for the aesthetic, with
cleaner lines defining a new design for a new century.

With a vintage look it is allowable if not advisable to mix styles. The centerpiece here is a table designed by **Joseph D'Urso** for
Knoll in the 1980s (*opposite*). It reflects his inclination for his designs to look more engineered than styled—which perfectly suits
the chairs. They were designed by **Josef Hoffmann** in 1904 for the Purkersdorf Sanatorium. They were designed for functionality
but also have the style of the Vienna Secession. The painting by James Nares gives a touch of modernity.

From the 1760s to the 1840s the decorative arts in Europe and North America were dominated by Neo-classicism and Classical revivals. Some designers and craftsmen favored Roman precedents, some Greek, some ancient Egyptian, and while there were brief periods in which oriental and Gothic styles were also looked to, because the sources of inspiration lay primarily in one large vocabulary of architecture and ornament—that of the Classical world—a broad stylistic coherence was conferred on the era. This was, however, in marked contrast to the middle and much of the second half of the 19th century—a period dominated by stylistic eclecticism. It is in the reaction to this diversification that the roots of 20th-century Modernism can be found.

Nineteenth-century eclecticism was essentially driven by economic and social developments. The second phase of the Industrial Revolution, and the attendant growth in international trade and domestic economies, gave rise to a rapidly expanding and increasingly affluent middle class. This, in turn, resulted in increased demand for bigger and more stylish homes to reflect their owners' newfound status. The surest way to secure that, it seemed, was to look to the past, to the prestigious styles of design and ornament that had hitherto been the preserve of the aristocratic and upper classes. Thus all manner of "historical-revival" styles began to appear, and the Classical revivals of earlier in the century now vied with revivals of medieval Gothic, 17th-century Baroque, and early

From left to right

Steam technology creates the sinuous, interlaced bentwood forms in **Thonet**'s shield-back chair of c.1885. 36.5in (92.5cm) high
★★ ★ ★ ★ ★

Although the influence of both traditional Middle Eastern and contemporary Art Nouveau forms are evident in **George Ohr**'s late 19th-century vase, the use of a mottled gun-metal and amber glaze with raspberry and green flashes lends the composition a prescient modernity. 8.25in (21cm) high
★★★★ ★ ★

1885

1890

18th-century Rococo. Moreover, as one contemporary observer noted, "it was not unusual to find a Medieval-Baronial dining room, a Louis XIV drawing room, a Rococo parlor, a Gothic library, and a Moresque boudoir under the one roof."

In some cases such historical eclecticism was aesthetically rather pleasing, if somewhat whimsical. However, in many more it was seriously diminished by a fusion or, more pertinently, a confusion of styles within individual rooms, and even within individual artifacts. Thus a "Louis-Revival" or "Old French" interior might combine elements of grand Baroque Louis XIV and curvaceous Rococo Louis XV with rectilinear Neo-classical Louis XVI styles. Similarly, a "reproduction" of an early 18th-century late Baroque vase might now be augmented with a plethora of overlaid, often highly colorful Rococo-style decoration that bore no relation to the simpler and more graceful aesthetics of the original piece. This garish over-ornamentation was often further fueled by the sheer volume of furnishings and decorative objects in a typical interior of the 1860s, '70s or '80s—a period of ostentatious display in which more, rather than less, equaled more.

Into this cluttered mix can be added a problem of quality: the increasing industrialization of manufacturing had facilitated a production boost to meet the higher levels of demand for home furnishings. However, the price to be paid for mass production often lay in a significant drop in standards, when compared to

From left to right

Traditional craftsmanship and machine production are combined in German designer **Richard Riemerschmid**'s iconic armchair of c.1900. 33.25in (84cm) high ★★ ☆ ☆ ☆ ☆

The rectilinear geometric breakaway by the Vienna Secession and the Wiener Werkstätte from the organic, curvilinear Art Nouveau is clearly evident in Austrian **Josef Hoffmann**'s white metal flower basket. 9.5in (24cm) high ★★ ☆ ☆ ☆ ☆

American cabinetmaker and designer **Charles Rohlfs**' oak hall chair pre-empts the pared-down simplicity of Modernism while tipping its hat, via hand-carved fretwork, to medieval Gothic and Scandinavian forms. 16.5in (42cm) wide ★★ ☆ ☆ ☆ ☆

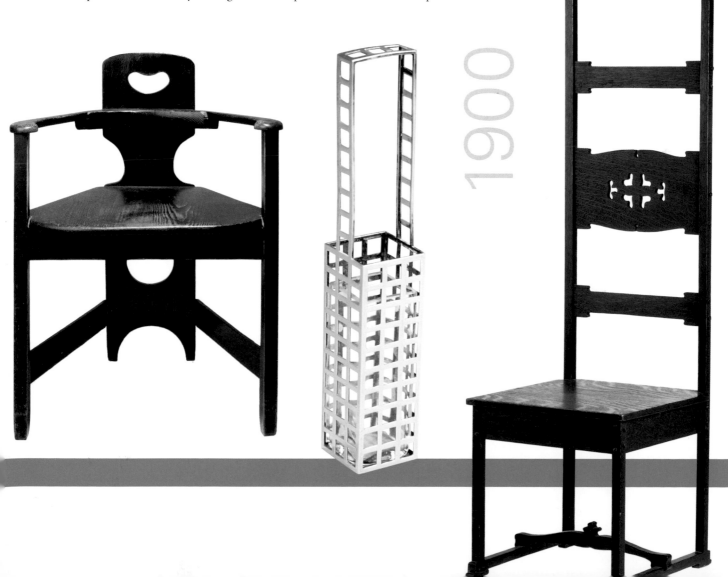

1900

traditionally handmade artifacts. It was this, in combination with the cluttered mix of oddly or badly reinterpreted historical styles, that proved the tipping point for many designers and craftsmen, and a series of reactions to it ensued—the first of significance being the Arts and Crafts movement.

Political and economic factors also played a part in the changing influences on design. The Crimean War, which probably caused 500,000 deaths, and resulting economic disruption forced many to re-evaluate the old order. Looking to the past came to be considered out-of-date. The new desire to look to the future, and to find new ways of doing things, was further boosted by scientific discoveries and advances in technology. As the 20th century dawned, the developed countries in the west were starting to experience the first shoots of Modernism, in social and technological terms, and these were often mirrored—or even preceded—by artistic achievements.

Founded by **William Morris**, the Arts and Crafts movement emerged in Britain in the 1860s and thrived throughout the late 19th century. Indeed, it survived in its country of origin into the 1930s. One of its enduring legacies to 20th-century Modernism lay not so much in the particular style its original proponents advocated—one largely derived from the medieval English and Gothic styles—but in the belief that decoration should be an integral part of an artifact rather than a superficial addition to it. This was a far more "purist"

From left to right

American **Gustav Stickley**'s early 20th-century oak-framed Morris armchair, named after **William Morris**, founder of the Arts and Crafts movement, combines traditional through-tenon carpentry that dates back to the Middle Ages with the pared-down, rectilinear simplicity of embryonic Modernism. 40in (124cm) high ★★★☆☆

Traditional eastern and Far Eastern imagery are infused in Italian **Carlo Bugatti**'s chair designs, as are early 20th-century preoccupations with geometric forms—the resulting fusion proving both modern and unique. 28in (72cm) high ★★★☆☆

1902

approach to design, and was echoed elsewhere in the ideas of the Glaswegian botanist and designer **Christopher Dresser**. While Dresser advocated looking at many different civilizations as sources of inspiration for design—notably Egyptian, Persian, Meso-American, and, especially, Japanese—underpinning it, and giving it an aesthetic coherence, was his view that real beauty lay in nature and, more specifically, in the linear simplicity and geometrical balance of plant forms. Dresser's publications, which included theories on interior decoration and the use of color and ornament, lay at the heart of what became the Aesthetic movement, and were to prove highly influential elsewhere. In the United States they were adopted by **Charles Eastlake**, who through his own publications did much gradually to render unfashionable over-furnished and over-ornamented "High Victorian" American parlors.

This re-emphasis on the beauty and the clarity of organic forms also flourished in Northern Europe from the 1880s, especially in France, through the Art Nouveau movement. Exemplified by the pioneering furniture, glass and ceramic designs of the Frenchman **Emile Gallé**, this distinctive style was characterized by stylized plant forms with an exaggerated and asymmetric curvaceousness that was positively Rococo-esque. Highly distinctive, Art Nouveau was to prove fashionable in Europe almost until the outbreak of World War I in 1914, and although far less evident in the United States, its floral and other

From left to right

While plant forms are clearly the primary inspiration for the form of this Art Nouveau vase by Belgian-born **Henry van de Velde**, the degree of abstraction in the design also points to a style beyond Art Nouveau. 11.25in (28.5cm) high ★★★★★★

During the early years of the 20th century the steamed bentwood furniture of the Gebrüder Thonet company gradually moved away from the overtly curvilinear forms of Art Nouveau towards more rectilinear geometric shapes. 41in (104cm) high ★★★★★★

1903

1904

plant-form imagery was reflected in some of the designs—most notably the decorative glass and glass lampshades—of **Louis Comfort Tiffany**. However, apart from its emphasis on the organic, Art Nouveau would not turn out to be prescient of Modernism. Indeed, its sinuous, stylized asymmetric curves were to be rejected by the latter in favor of far more rectilinear precedents.

The overtly rectilinear aesthetic that emerged during the late 19th century was, at its heart, a celebration of the inherent symmetry—as opposed to asymmetry—that could be identified in nature. It emerged most influentially in the now iconic designs of the Glaswegian **Charles Rennie Mackintosh** and the Glasgow School, and in those Austrian artists and architects, including **Joseph Maria Olbrich**, **Josef Hoffmann**, and **Koloman Moser**, who in 1897 formed the Vienna Secession as a rejection of eclectic historicism in art and design; in the United States, their equivalents were to be found in the Arts and Crafts furniture designs of **Charles Rohlfs**, in the Arts and Crafts–driven Craftsmen movement championed by **Gustav Stickley**, in the related Mission Style and, perhaps above all, in the pioneering work of the architect **Frank Lloyd Wright**. Their particular sources of decorative inspiration varied—for example, Japanese is to the fore in the designs of Mackintosh and Lloyd Wright, while medieval Gothic resonates in Rohlfs'. However, they are all bound by a clarity and symmetry of line in which extraneous Victorian ornament has all but been dispensed with, and replaced by an inherent sense of light and space and, indeed, a greater sense of functionality.

From left to right

A beechwood-stained-to-mahogany, drum-shaped table manufactured by J.&J. Kohn and originally designed with matching chairs by **Josef Hoffmann** for the Cabaret Fledermaus in Vienna. 29in (72.5cm) high ★★★★★

Cylindrical shapes—bowl, stem, and foot—dominate this Austrian wine glass designed by **Otto Prutscher**, and are complemented by other recurring geometric forms in the blue overlay and cut-glass decoration. 8.5in (21cm) high ★★★★★

A Jugendstil casket, attributed to **Josef Hoffmann**, seems very modern. The stripes of blackened wood give a distinctly Art Deco feel, although it was designed in 1910. 9in (22cm) wide ★★★★★

1906   1907   1910

By the end of the 19th century, the aesthetics of 20th-century Modernism were thus well on their way and, crucially, were given further impetus by the resolution of an artistic–industrial conundrum. The Arts and Crafts movement had emerged in part as a rejection of mechanized forms of production and the attendant problems of poor quality. Unfortunately, its solution—a return to high standards of manufacture by trained and skilled hands—equated to lower and more expensive output, and thereby rendered many Arts and Crafts artifacts elitist and the preserve of those with deep pockets. This was no way forward for populist design, given the rapidly expanding and increasingly style-hungry populations on both sides of the Atlantic.

Fortunately, some far-sighted and entrepreneurial artists and designers took this on board. The embracing of gradually improving industrial technology by Dr. Christopher Dresser in England, by Gustav Stickley and the Craftsmen movement in the United States, by the "bentwood" furniture pioneer **Michael Thonet** in Austria, and by design cooperatives such as the Wiener Werkstätte (established 1903 in Vienna by Josef Hoffmann and Koloman Moser), and the Deutsher Werkbund (founded 1907 in Munich by **Hermann Muthesius**, **Peter Behrens**, **Richard Riemerschmid** and Joseph Maria Olbrich), marked the union of artistic integrity and innovative design with high-quality machine production. And that, together with the rectilinear aesthetic, laid a clear path to the industrial Modernist designs of the 20th century.

From left to right

A tall American Beauty vase, hand-hammered and patinated in sheet copper at the Roycroft Arts and Crafts community workshops in East Aurora, New York. 21in (53.5cm) high ★★ ★ ★ ★

A pair of **Josef Hoffmann** mahogany barrel chairs, designed for the Weiner Werkstätte. Designed in 1914, they preceded by 10 years the popular style of the 1920s. 35.5in (90cm) high ★★★ ★ ★

1914

Designers who led the way

The work of four individuals set the tone for the first modern designs from the late 19th century. Their designs resonate with a more modern approach.

Christopher Dresser

Scottish-born Christopher Dresser is said to be the first industrial designer. By the end of the 19th century he was renowned for promoting design reform and modern manufacturing techniques. His designs for wallpaper, textiles, ceramics, glass, furniture, and metalware were considered radical in their time, and still appear modern today. He studied botany at the new Government School of Design, and his belief that plants had a simplicity of form and clear function influenced his work. Japanese design had an effect on his work following a visit in 1876. But pieces also show influences from Egyptian forms, antiquity and feudal Europe.

Traditional Peruvian forms inspired **Christopher Dresser**'s bridge-handle-spouted, streaked- and dribble-glazed ceramic pitcher designed c.1893 for Ault & Co. 7in (17cm) high ★★★★★

c.1893

1870

Thonet

In 1859 German cabinetmaker Michael Thonet and his four sons perfected a mechanized process for creating bentwood furniture, and so pioneered standardized furniture. Thonet had begun his experiments with bentwood in the 1830s, and he developed a revolutionary process where lengths of beechwood were boiled or steamed in water, then bent into long, curved rods to be used as frames. The resulting chair was light and flexible, inexpensive, and durable, and did away with the need for hand-carved joints. Thonet's landmark 1959 chair had flowing curves, and was devoid of ornament. The firm Gebrüder Thonet received international patents for the process.

Mechanized steaming techniques facilitated mass-produced curvaceous Rococo-esque and, later, Art Nouveau furniture by **Thonet**. 44in (111.75cm) wide ★★★★★

1902

Charles Rennie Mackintosh

Charles Rennie Mackintosh trained as an architect, and by c.1900 he was a leading exponent of the Glasgow School style—a version of Art Nouveau with some Celtic influences. The Scotsman is now world renowned for his architecture, furniture, and graphic and textile designs. He had a unique style, was appreciative of Japanese design and was influenced by the designers of the Wiener Werkstätte, who similarly drew inspiration from him. He is best known for his architectural commissions for Glasgow School of Art, and for Hill House, in Helensburgh, west of Glasgow. Mackintosh designed detailed integrated interiors for both.

Mackintosh's 292 Hill House chair is an elegant rectilinear composition of wooden slats and poles and upholstered seating. 55.5in (141cm) high ★★★★★ 1973 reissue, ★★★★★ original

Frank Lloyd Wright

The American architect, designer, and writer Frank Lloyd Wright studied architecture and engineering. He believed that a house had its own "grammar," which influenced every aspect of it. The style of architecture he developed at his Chicago practice became the cornerstone of the Prairie School. The houses he built around the city were inspired by the surrounding prairie and Japanese design. His reputation as a furniture designer is largely based on the pieces he designed for these homes. His early interiors were in the Arts and Crafts style, with his high-backed chairs probably influenced by British examples by designers such as Charles Rennie Mackintosh.

Fashioned from mortise-and-tenoned oak, augmented with a leather-covered seat pad, and characteristically dominated by rectangular forms, this chair was originally designed by **Frank Lloyd Wright** for the Hillside Home School, Wisconsin. 40in (102cm) high ★★★★★★

1904

DECO WORLD

1918–1945

Between the two World Wars, a diverse range of
design styles developed, but one thing they all had
in common was the desire to be "modern."

Eileen Gray's Non Conformist chair took the Art Deco aesthetic of comfort
and modernity and gave it a twist. She explained the unusual form, as
follows: "An armrest was omitted in order to leave the lady more freedom
in movement and to allow it to bend forward or to turn to the other side
unrestricted." c.1926 30in (76cm) high 1970s example ★ ★ ★ ★

A Break with the Past

As the world returned to normal following World War I, society developed a desire for modernity. A number of design styles developed that have been given the name Art Deco. Some feature African or Egyptian iconography, or elements of the influential art movement Cubism; others celebrate the speed of the motor car, the elegance of French design or the excitement of the Jazz Age and flapper girls. They may be made from luxurious materials such as ebony and ivory or the latest innovations such as chrome and plastic. The one thing they all have in common is a rejection of the past and a desire for adventure, leisure, and luxury as a reaction to the horrors of the trenches.

René Lalique managed to take pressed glass and make it art. This Nivernais press-molded glass vase embodies the period with its bright color and geometric design. c.1927 6.5in (16.5cm) high ★★ ☆ ☆ ☆ ☆

A ceramic figure of dancing girls, designed by **Stefan Dakon** for Goldscheider. The stylized figures wear typically revealing costumes. 1930s 13.5in (34cm) high ★★ ☆ ☆ ☆ ☆

A chair with geometric seat cushions and elegant tapering legs by **Maxime Old**, with original red leather upholstery. 1930s 36in (91.5cm) high ★★ ☆ ☆ ☆ ☆

The discovery of King Tutankhamen's tomb in the 1920s inspired forms of Egyptian decoration. The stools in this room (*opposite*) were made in Cairo, styled after stools found in the tomb.

In the decorative arts the 21 years spanning the end of World War I in 1918 and the beginning of World War II in 1939 are primarily associated with the Art Deco style. The term Art Deco was derived retrospectively from the Exposition Internationale des Arts Décoratifs et Industriels Moderne, which had been held in Paris in 1925. A showcase for architects, designers, and manufacturers working in all aspects of the decorative arts, it proved hugely successful in disseminating internationally cutting-edge design. However, despite the fact that it gave its name to inter-war style, there was nothing stylistically monolithic about the period. Indeed, the "Deco World" drew on numerous sources of decorative inspiration—some new, some old—and in many respects can be usefully viewed as a symbolic struggle between the flower and the machine.

With roots in the late 19th and early 20th century—in the Aesthetic and the Arts and Crafts and Craftsmen movements; in the artist-craftsmen co-operatives of the Vienna Secession, the Wiener Werkstätte, and the Deutscher Werkbund; in the work of individual architects and designers such as **Michael Thonet**, **Charles Rennie Mackintosh**, and **Frank Lloyd Wright**—it was the Modern movement that was to provide the most formidable aesthetic of the Deco World. It was, moreover, further fueled by new directions in fine art. Cubism, which emerged in the first decade of the 20th century and was, arguably, the most influential art movement of the century, inspired many Modernist architects and designers, particularly in its dissolution and reconstruction of three-dimensional forms using simple geometric shapes, and also in how it allowed diverse elements in a composition to be superimposed, or made transparent, or penetrate one another, all while retaining their spatial relationships. Emerging around the same time, in Italy, the avant-garde Futurism movement promoted an urban rather than a rural future, in which the cities, stripped of unnecessary decorative embellishments, would be efficient machines. This also informed and sat well with Modernist projections, as did Futurism's celebration of speed and technology, the motor car and the airplane, which collectively conjured up imagery that would come to epitomize the Art Deco style of the late 1920s and the 1930s.

Given substantial further impetus by the German architect **Walter Gropius'** establishment, in 1919, of the Staatliches Bauhaus—a school of arts and crafts simply and better-known as just Bauhaus—Modernism thus continued stripping away superfluous decorative embellishments to make form the primary object of aesthetic admiration, and that all-important form was to be determined solely by function. In practice this, in most cases, meant unadorned,

The work of the Wiener Werkstätte featured many of the rectilinear devices seen in Art Deco design. This poster advertising their work features the group's geometric logo and a typical design for a metal vase by **Josef Hoffmann** (*above left*).

Charles Rennie Mackintosh's rectilinear chair designs pre-dated many similar Art Deco pieces (*left*). He designed this mahogany ladderback chair for the guest bedroom of 78 Derngate, Northampton, England, the home of W. J. Basset-Lowke. The stepped ladderback extends to the feet, and the legs are supported by two stretchers at the sides and one at the front. The upholstery is also woven with a geometric pattern. c.1917 34.25in (87cm) high ★★★ ☆ ☆

Art Deco designers including **Jean Dunand** designed rooms for the 1925 Exposition Internationale des Arts Décoratifs et Industriels Modernes in Paris. Jean Dunand's lacquered smoking room at the Ambassade Française featured a geometric stepped ceiling and boxy tables and chairs (*left*). The Ambassade Française was organized by the Societé des Artistes Decorateurs and consisted of 25 rooms arranged around a three-sided court.

Stylized Egyptian papyrus flowers and olive branches decorate this cameo-glass vase by Daum Frères (*below*). It is made from colorless glass with milky powder inclusions and a vitrified blue outer layer acid-etched with the design. 1926 11.5in (29.5cm) high
★★ ★ ★ ★ ★

rectilinear-angular geometric forms in which the industrial origins and process of manufacture were highlighted, and within that considerable emphasis was placed on the quality and, indeed, the texture of the materials employed—concrete, glass, and steel (often chromed and tubular) being especially favored.

Underpinning all of this, in an era of increasingly sophisticated industrial manufacturing, was the desire to make not just the city but the home—in the words of one of Modernism's leading lights, the Swiss-French architect and designer **Le Corbusier**—"a machine for living in." This rationalist, streamlined approach to design was exciting stuff, and pointed to a bright new future—an especially appealing prospect in the 1920s and '30s after the terrible privations of World War I. However, there were other new and exciting influences that had emerged during the first two decades of the 20th century, and these had also fed into many of the Deco designs on display at the 1925 Exposition in Paris.

Chief among these influences was the "Tutmania" that followed the excavation of the ancient Egyptian pharaoh Tutankhamen's tomb in 1922. The glittering opulence of the gilded, bejeweled, and polychrome-painted artifacts that emerged (and which were exhibited around the world) kindled a substantial revival across the decorative arts of all things ancient Egyptian. Similarly, the near-concurrent excavation of Aztec tombs promoted considerable interest in indigenous Central American architecture, art and ornament. It was, however,

The risqué costumes and sheer exuberance of the dancers at the Ballets Russes inspired many artists. **Demêtre Chiparus**'s Dourga figure shows a theatrical dancer in full Ballets Russes costume (*right*). The gilt and silvered-bronze figure has a hand-carved ivory face and hands and is raised on a variegated cream-and-brown onyx decorative base. c.1925 13in (34cm) ★ ★ ★ ★ ☆

Seen here in performance (*below*), the Ballets Russes de Monte Carlo, which formed in 1937 in the aftermath of artistic differences between co-founders of the original Ballets Russes, provided, like its Paris-based predecessor, significant inspiration to designers working in the inter-war Art Deco style. The primary vehicle for this was its colorful, flamboyant, and often exotic sets and costumes.

Sergei Diaghilev's ballet company, the Ballets Russes, which delivered perhaps the most innovative designs of the period. Parisian-based, and performing throughout Europe and North and South America from 1909 to 1929, the extraordinary sets and costumes—which provided the backdrop to Nijinsky and Pavlova dancing to music by Debussy, Prokofiev, Ravel, Strauss, and Stravinsky—were conceived by, among others, Léon Bakst, Georges Braque, Pablo Picasso, Henri Matisse, Salvador Dalí, and Coco Chanel.

This exciting and colorful new Art Deco imagery, like glittering Tutmania, sat well in the vibrant and optimistic post-war Jazz Age of the 1920s. However, after the Wall Street Crash of 1929, and set against a background of the great economic Depression that followed and the attendant rise of Fascist and Socialist dictatorships in Europe, these profusions of shape and color lost ground to increasingly minimalist and monochromatic Modernism. As they did so, the eminent French designer **Paul Iribe** observed: "[we have] sacrificed the flower on the altar of the machine." Inevitably, however, a stylistic reaction to that would, in due course, ensue.

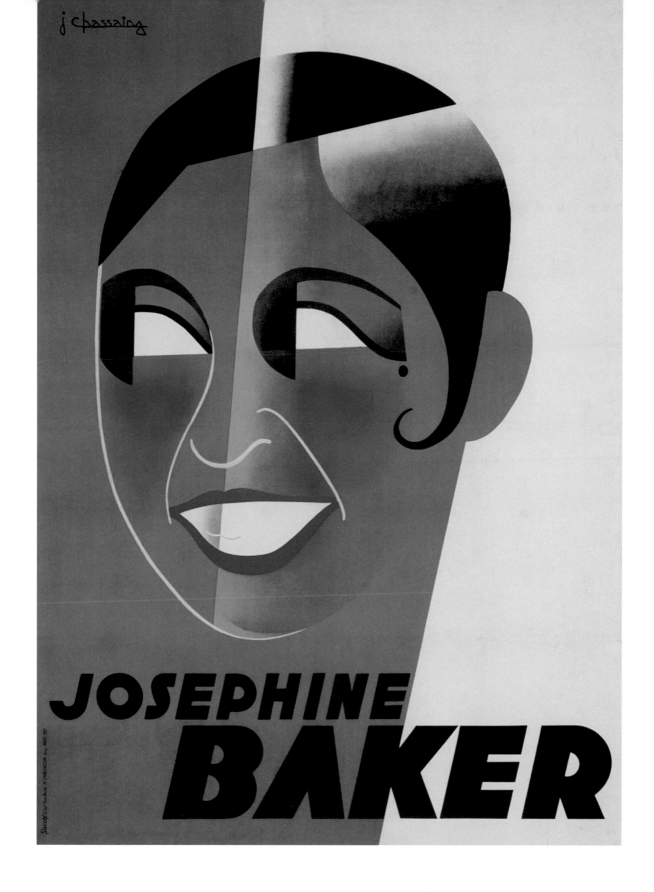

The highly stylized designs of **Jean Chassaing** are emblematic of the Art Deco movement. This is his best-known design and shows the actress Josephine Baker, using geometric blocks of color and incorporating the background color of the paper into the design. 1931 61.5in (156cm) high ★ ★ ★ ☆ ☆

GRAND PRIX
1925

MAGASIN DU
MEUBLE

AUBUCHERON

GRAPHIC AND DECORATIVE

Stylized patterns—many of them geometric—are some of the hallmarks of the Art Deco style. Elements such as the sunburst or sunray motifs were taken from ancient Aztec, Inca, and Native American art, while the exoticism of African tribal masks found its way into designs for wall masks and vases. Other popular motifs were stylized flowers, often depicted in swags or baskets, stepped and architectural forms as part of the structure and the decoration of a building, stylized animals such as deer and borzoi hounds, and the female form. Bold color harmonies were often used to enhance these designs, whether painted on or created from exotic wooden and ivory inlays on furniture.

opposite, clockwise from top left The square-section dark wooden frames of these club chairs create a severe outline that is slightly softened by the upholstery. / A small glimpse of **Clarice Cliff**'s bold geometrics that were revolutionary in the 1920s. / **Jean Cocteau** was among the artists who embraced the Art Deco movement and enjoyed the freedom of working in more than one medium. This plate, with its intricate design of stylized faces and leaves, is among the pieces he designed. / The advertising poster designed by **Cassandre** for Au Burcheron is striking, with strong blue and black lines radiating from a lumberjack and falling tree.

right The decoration of walls, doors, and many items of furniture at Charleston—a country house in Sussex, England, and home from 1916 to the literary and artistic Bloomsbury Group—was inspired by Italian fresco and Post-Impressionist paintings. The fireplace overmantel here, like the coal box below, was painted by Duncan Grant in 1932–34.

The line of beauty

Advertising posters designed by **Cassandre** feature strong geometric motifs. This example, for train-operating company Chemin de Fer du Nord, has a bold compass design incorporating sophisticated airbrushing, the "N" at the head of the compass reinforcing the "N" of "Nord" in the poster typography. 1929 39.25in (99.5cm) high ★★ ☆ ☆ ☆

One of the most notable innovations of the Art Deco movement was the use of graphic patterns and layouts to decorate ceramics, create eye-catching posters, and make the most of one of the new materials of the age—Bakelite.

The style had been pioneered by designers at the Wiener Werkstätte and the Bauhaus, and was also used by poster artists such as **Jean Chassaing**, **Edward McKnight Kauffer**, and **Albert Fuss**. Art Deco typefaces usually featured stylized geometric letters, and this geometry can be seen in overall design of some posters. The work of Jean Chassaing, **Paul Colin**, **Willem Ten Broek**, and Albert Fuss shows the influence of Cubism and exhibit a geometric balance and startling use of color in its composition. Posters advertising ocean liners are highly stylized, while those for the stage may even caricature the stars they promote.

In contrast, **Boris Lovet-Lorski** combined abstract beams of light with sensuous female figures and geometric lettering. **Jean Dupas** used a unique style to depict his subjects—particularly women—in an idealized androgynous way. Edward McKnight Kauffer, the leading British graphic artist of the time, was influenced by Futurism and Cubism, but the style of his work depended on the client and could use strict geometry or a more romantic line.

The art of ancient Egypt also played its part in the new graphic lexicon. The riches discovered by Howard Carter in Tutankhamen's tomb in 1922, news of which traveled the world, inspired designers to shape and decorate ceramics, glass, jewelry, metalware, and furniture with pharaohs' heads, hieroglyphics, scarabs, pyramids, and cobras. The bold blue, green, red, and gold they used mimicked the colors that had been found hidden for centuries in the tomb.

Factories such as the British Carlton Ware adapted existing forms to the new style, for example a Chinese-style ginger jar was given a sphinx knop and decorated with hieroglyphs and other hand-painted details.

The ceramics designed by **Charles Catteau** and others at Boch Frères in Belgium feature geometric decoration with an historic twist. Many of the factory's vases feature a crackled glaze that deliberately gives the illusion of an ancient ceramic discovered at an archaeological dig.

Often, the bold, graphic shapes, patterns, and forms were taken from exotic Aztec, Inca, or Native American iconography and reinterpreted for the modern world. Sunbursts and zigzags are an example of this. Color combinations were also important—black, yellow, and green or red, cream, and black were seen as having African roots, as did the use of contrasting pale and dark earth tones.

British designers **Clarice Cliff** and **Susie Cooper** used striking abstract patterns, as well as some geometric ones. These were revolutionary at the time. Some tablewares featured solid bands of as many as five or six colors, which give the work a more random, bold feel.

Animals were also depicted in a modern, stylized way. At the Carter, Stabler & Adams factory in Poole, Dorset (later Poole Pottery), **Truda Carter**'s designs depicted leaping deer surrounded by stylized flowers and foliage. Other factories treated pumas, other big cats, and the fashionable borzoi hounds in the same way.

Ceramic figures often interpreted the female form as stylized, sleek, slim, and athletic, with boyish cropped hair and wearing revealing costumes. The Lenci

Egyptian motifs allowed opportunities for creating repeating patterns. Carlton Ware's Tutankhamen ginger jar and cover are decorated with gilt Egyptian scenes and motifs over a royal blue ground (*above*). c.1920s 13in (34cm) high ★★ ★ ★ ★ ★

Rich colors and gilding are used to create a stylized design on this Carlton Ware Egyptian Fan temple jar and cover (*right*). It is decorated with a bold fan motif alongside towering flowers. c.1930s 7in (18cm) high ★ ★ ★ ★ ★

Bold hand-painted repeating designs are a feature of **Clarice Cliff**'s work (*below*). This Double V–A shape 269 vase was decorated with a band of stylized leaves and chevrons between black, orange, and green banding. The base bears the Bizarre mark. c.1929 6in (15cm) high ★ ★ ★ ★ ★

Susie Cooper's highly stylized Mountain and Moons pattern uses dramatic color contrasts to enhance the design. These plates were part of the range designed for Grays Pottery in the late 1920s. 5.5in (14cm) wide ★ ★ ★ ★ ★

The stylized gazelles, stepped black vitriolite base and frosted glass stepped shade of this table lamp mimic the work of **René Lalique** and are typical Art Deco forms. 1930s 8.75in (22cm) high ★ ★ ★ ★ ★

The overlapping fish that decorate this cased yellow glass **Lalique** Poissons vase are enhanced by the addition of a sepia patina. c.1921 9.5in (23.5cm) high ★ ★ ★ ☆ ☆ ☆

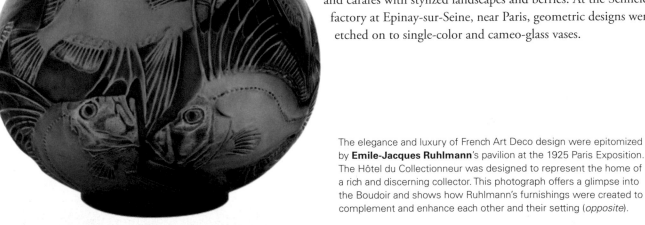

factory in Turin, Italy, depicted languorous, modern women indulging in smoking and sunbathing, and often nude. Meanwhile, the German factory at Katzhutte showed sleek and fashionable women in elegant poses.

Designers such as **Dorothea Charol** and **Clare Weiss** at the Rosenthal porcelain factory in Bavaria created graceful and elegant figures that reflected the modern taste for exotic dancers and hand-painted tablewares painted with stylized plants and trees. All their wares contrast bold colors with a white or ivory base.

In contrast, while factories such as Meissen in Germany and Sèvres in France did make some Art Deco pieces, the majority of their output during the 1920s and '30s was traditional in style. At Meissen **Max Esser** created groups of mythological animals, while his colleague **Paul Scheurich** produced elegant yet demure female figures. Sèvres made pieces in the Modernist tradition, mostly thanks to Georges Lechavallier-Chevignard, who became its director in 1920. He commissioned designers including **Emile-Jacques Ruhlmann**, **Henri Rapin**, and **Suzanne Lalique** to create vases and other decorative wares. The sculptor **François Pompon** re-created his celebrated bronzes of creatures—such as his famous polar bear—in earthenware, to great success. Other French ceramics firms, including Limoges, soon followed suit and commissioned designers to help them to refresh their wares.

The Cowan factory near Cleveland, Ohio, employed artists including **Viktor Schreckengost**, **Margaret Postgate**, **Alexander Blazys**, and **A. Drexler Jacobson** to create stylized figural "flower frogs" and figures or real or mythological beasts as well as women, such as the dancer Gilda Gray.

The taste for African-inspired design extended to sculpture. The metal designs created by the Austrian firm Hagenauer Werkstätte were broadly inspired by two art forms: African and western. The African animal and stick-figure figurines reflect the popular fascination with colonialism and have stylized bodies and sculptural poses. Some of the high-end pieces include wall masks that evoke the work of **Pablo Picasso**.

The bold Bakelite bangles many women wore up to their elbows had African roots, as did the large bead necklaces made from the same material. In the 1920s and '30s Bakelite and other plastics revolutionized homewares as they were ideal for molding into the latest geometric shapes and—since they were relatively affordable—found their way into many homes.

Fashionable glass wares were also decorated with graphic, geometric designs. The French artist **Marcel Goupy** painted vases and carafes with stylized landscapes and berries. At the Schneider factory at Epinay-sur-Seine, near Paris, geometric designs were etched on to single-color and cameo-glass vases.

The elegance and luxury of French Art Deco design were epitomized by **Emile-Jacques Ruhlmann**'s pavilion at the 1925 Paris Exposition. The Hôtel du Collectionneur was designed to represent the home of a rich and discerning collector. This photograph offers a glimpse into the Boudoir and shows how Ruhlmann's furnishings were created to complement and enhance each other and their setting (*opposite*).

This bedroom designed by **Emile-Jacques Ruhlmann** for the 1925 Paris Exposition shows how he envisaged a complete interior.

The subtle bow front and mirror-cut mahogany crotch veneers of this rosewood and mahogany *secretaire* show attention to detail and respect for traditional craftsmanship. This piece, by **Léon Jallot**, was exhibited at the 1925 Paris Exposition. c.1925 34.75in (88cm) wide ★★★★☆☆

The Classical movement

In France modern tastes collided with traditional decorations to create interiors and furnishings that brought classic styles and techniques up to date. The results exhibit high standards of craftsmanship, exotic materials, and an elegance that recalls the designs of the 18th century. Many of these designs had their foundation in the Art Nouveau style, but the flowing lines and naturalistic decoration became more controlled and restrained, with graceful proportions and stylized motifs.

Many fashionable interiors were created by furniture designers such as **Emile-Jacques Ruhlmann**, **Jules Leleu**, and **Léon** and **Maurice Jallot**. They became known as *artiste décorateurs* and created entire interior schemes featuring their own luxurious work. Ruhlmann and his French contemporaries created some of the most technically advanced and expensive Art Deco furniture and decorative objects. These found a ready market in France and with wealthy Americans who traveled to Paris to discover the latest fashions and pastimes.

Furniture was made from exotic—and expensive—materials such as mahogany, amboyna, ebony, and rosewood. Ruhlmann used time-consuming and expensive decorative techniques such as carving, veneers, and inlays of tortoiseshell, mother-of-pearl, shagreen (imitation sharkskin) and ivory to enhance his simple, stylized, abstract pieces. Highly polished wooden surfaces were often contrasted with richly decorated upholstery.

Paul Follot combined exotic materials with simple, traditional shapes used as recently as the 18th and 19th centuries and as far back as ancient Greece and

Restrained flat cabriole legs support the top of this **Sue et Mare** bird's-eye maple and mahogany demi-lune side table. The broad cross-banded top sits above a thumb-molded edge and features a single frieze drawer. c.1925 48in (122cm) wide ★★★☆☆☆

Rome, to create Art Deco furnishings and interiors. The decorations he used included a basket of flowers—a motif that became synonymous with Art Deco designs. The furnishings he designed before World War I tend to be more richly decorated than those made after 1920.

The Neo-classical style of the early 20th century can be seen in the work of **Louis Sue** and **André Mare**. They designed furniture and interiors under their own names and as the Compagnie des Arts Français. The pieces they designed tend to be on a grand scale, with gilding, lacquers, and extravagant cast-metal fittings.

The mixture of simple forms and contrasting colors, rectangular club chairs and simple tables used by Parisian **Jean-Michel Frank** continue to influence modern interiors today. Frank was one of the most influential decorators in the city between the two world wars. His understated designs featured vellum-covered walls and furniture made from exotic woods and leather upholstery with minimal decoration but embellished with mother-of-pearl, parchment, lacquer, or ivory.

Frank collaborated with designers including **Adolphe Chanaux** and **Jean Dunand** and commissioned artists and craftsmen including **Alberto** and **Diego Giacometti**, **Salvador Dalí**, **Emilio Terry**, and **Christian Bérard** to contribute a range of designs. He also worked for the fashion designer **Elsa Schiaparelli**.

The French taste for furniture based on 18th-century designs and decorated with complex veneers and parquetry, subtle carving and a mix of exotic woods inspired the New York designer **Eugene Schoen**. His work is often mistaken for

Contrasting colored woods are used to create a rectilinear design for this rosewood and amboyna sideboard attributed to **Jules Leleu**. It has three cabinet doors enclosing interior shelves. The center door has a clear glass panel, and the doors at either end have horizontal chrome handles. 78.5in (199cm) wide ★ ★ ☆ ☆ ☆ ☆

Geometric marquetry decoration enhances the front of this plum-pudding mahogany, ebonized dressing table by **Maurice Dufrêne**. It has a folding triple beveled mirror above a central tabouret flanked by four tear-shaped drawers. 1921–22 52.75in (134cm) wide ★ ★ ☆ ☆ ☆ ☆

Square glass panels make up the geometric shade of this classic Art Deco lamp by **Desney**. The silver base adds to the simplicity of the form. c.1925 5in (13cm) high ★ ★ ☆ ☆ ☆ ☆

Neo-classical elements of the Empire style influenced some Art Deco interiors. This office (*opposite*) pays homage to these with a 1930s **Frits Henningsen** armchair upholstered in midnight-blue velvet set in front of a vintage **Jean-Michel Frank** desk with a glazed porcelain table lamp by **Svend Hammershøi**. The **Märta Måås-Fjetterström** rug dates from the 1940s.

Biblical imagery inspired the decoration of this **Jean Mayodon** vase (*below left*). It shows Adam and Eve with three snakes, and has a wooden base. The restrained palette and artistic style are typical of his work. 1930s 22.5in (57cm) high ★★★☆☆☆

Four Classical face masks adorn this pâte-de-verre vase by **François-Emile Décorchement** (*below center*). The glass is enhanced by streaks and swirls of beige and brown inclusions to create a marbled effect. 1919 5.25in (13.5cm) high ★★☆☆☆☆

A unique **Jean Mayodon** earthenware vase, glazed with turquoise craquelure glaze and gilding and hand-painted with a Classical-style scene of a nymph riding a seahorse (*below right*). The vase is further decorated with gilding to the rim and base. c.1935 9.5in (24cm) high ★★☆☆☆☆

that of his French contemporaries, but was made on the other side of the Atlantic using the same traditional techniques and elegant forms.

While wealthy customers commissioned pieces from high-end Parisian designers and decorators, those with more modest means could buy similar pieces by lesser manufacturers. By the 1920s the Belgian firm De Coene Frères was the largest furniture manufacturer in the country and—following the 1925 Paris Exhibition—went from making simple, provincial furniture to making pieces in the French Art Deco taste. The furniture is of a high quality and uses expensive materials including macassar ebony and ivory.

A more conservative version of the French style was favored in the U.K. **Ray Hille**, the daughter of the founder of the London-based firm Hille, was disappointed with the British furniture shown at the 1925 Paris Exposition. She saw the commercial possibilities of producing furniture in the French taste, and, following visits to Paris, she designed furniture—often inspired by the work of Paul Follot—that was made from blond wood or with exotic veneers.

Similar pieces were made by another London firm; Epstein Furniture. It produced custom-made furniture—particularly dining-room suites—decorated with burr maple, walnut, or sycamore veneers.

The trend for reinterpreting traditional designs and techniques in a modern way extended to glassmakers and ceramicists. French glassmaker **François-Emile Décorchemont** used the pâte-de-verre technique—where glass powder is heated in a mold to melt and shape it—to make thick-walled vases and bowls in traditional shapes but decorated with geometric Art Deco motifs. His work was exhibited at the 1925 Paris Exposition. He created textured exteriors, smooth interiors and veined and streaky colored decoration made with metallic oxides.

The French painter, interior designer and ceramicist **Jean Mayodon** made a unique series of vases, bowls and plates in simple forms but decorated with Neo-classical and mythological figures in the Art Deco style. He used muted colors and semi-matt glazes with crackled finishes and highlighted with gilding. He was also commissioned to make large-scale sculptural pieces for the ocean liner *Normandie*, among others.

Demêtre Chiparus

Demêtre Chiparus (1886–1947) was a Romanian Art Deco sculptor who lived and worked in Paris. In 1909 he went to Italy, where he attended the classes of Italian sculptor **Raffaello Romanelli**. In 1912 he traveled to Paris to attend the Ecole des Beaux Arts to pursue his art in the classes of **Antonin Mercié** and **Jean Boucher**. His most prestigious work was produced from the early 1920s.

Chiparus is known for the exquisite and subtly sensual modeling of the female (and also male) form. There is also the high quality of the casting, done at the prestigious Parisian foundries of Edmond Etling & Cie, and Les Neveux de J. Lehmann. And thirdly there is the exceptional decoration: the bronze and ivory (a combination known as chryselephantine) figure of the revue dancer based on Queen Semiramis is typical in its fabulous gilt, silvered, and enameled surface, and its stunning onyx and marble base. It is also typical of the Art Deco sculptors' fascination with the ancients. Semiramis is the Greek name for the Assyrian queen Sammuramat. Her accomplishments are said to have been founding Babylon, building the famous Hanging Gardens, the conquest of the entire Middle East, and invading Kush and India.

Above all these desirable characteristics, however, is the fact that Chiparus successfully encapsulated in his dancers the spirit, the essence of a most distinctive age. He was inspired by **Sergei Diaghilev**'s innovative and colorful Ballets Russes and by the sexually liberated French theatrical revues such as Les Folies Bergère. He was also captivated by the rediscovery of ancient Egyptian art—the tomb of the Boy King, Pharaoh Tutankhamen had been excavated in 1922. Chiparus's dancers appear to personify that most glamorous of eras and that most distinctive of styles: 1920s Art Deco.

Other notable examples of his work have included his Russian Dancers, modeled on Nijinsky and Ida Rubinstein in *Scheherazade*, from the Ballets Russes, and his chorus line of five dancers, known as Les Girls, which sold for over $500,000.

There were many other notable sculptors who embodied the dynamism of the Art Deco movement. **Bruno Zach**, who worked in Vienna, specialized in exotic and sometimes erotic subjects. **Ferdinand Preiss**, who worked in Berlin, is best known for his depiction of naturalistic 1920s women from the sporting and theatrical world. **Josef Lorenzl**, who worked in Vienna, was captivated by the female form and produced many bronze and chryselephantine sculptures of shapely dancing girls with long, elegant legs. **Erté** (Romain de Tirtoff) was a Russian-born artist who worked in Paris. He was a multi-talented designer who said, "Art Deco is the confluence of Cubism and Art Nouveau."

These Art Deco sculptures were highly desirable when they were produced and are still prized today, therefore they are expensive. There were copies produced at the time in less expensive materials, such as spelter and ivorine (a type of plastic). Although not of the same quality as the originals, these copies can be used to successfully create this very distinctive look at a fraction of the price.

An **Erté** sculpture stands atop an American Empire console (*right*).

A bronze Egyptian Dancer figure wears traditional costume picked out in cold-painted gilt and enamel. 1925 29in (73cm) ★★★★★★

The costume of this bronze and ivory Ballets Russes Hindu Dancer is enhanced by cold painted, silvered and enamel decoration. 1925 23.5in (60cm) high ★★★★★★

The revealing costume of the rare Dancer with a Scarf figure is typical of the risqué designs of the time. 1925 26.5in (67.5cm) ★★★★★★

Chiparus created an exotic costume for this Syrian Dancer figure. Her static pose contrasts with the dancing figure depicted on the base. 1925 13in (34cm) ★★★★★★

Demure designs such as this Innocence figure are less popular with collectors, but show **Chiparus'** skill at depicting folds of fabric. 1925 10in (25cm) ★★★★★★

A chryselephantine (bronze and ivory) figure of a revue dancer representing Queen Semiramis on an onyx and marble base. c.1925 26.4in (67cm) high ★★★★★★

Influential pieces

Daring designs created from expensive materials characterize much
Art Deco design. Ivory was used in the place of exotic woods to
veneer furniture or as intricate inlays. It was also combined with
bronze to create stylized figures of exotic dancers wearing revealing
costumes. Glass was engraved or molded with repeating designs,
some of them geometric, others of stylized leaves, figures, or animals.
Scenes or motifs from classical mythology also feature as designs
for ceramics or as decorative supports for furniture. Symmetry was
essential to the success of some designs, particularly the fountain
motif seen on many lampshades, perfume bottles, and fabrics. While
the inspiration for many of these may have been traditional, the
result was truly modern.

Alexandre Kelety was the master of
depicting the flow of the dance. This Pierrot
and his ballerina partner in classic bronze and
ivory are engrossed in the dance (*left*). He
has intriguingly removed her mask. 1925 19in
(49cm) ★★★ ☆ ☆

Luxury materials were an essential element
of many Art Deco pieces. This **Osvaldo
Borsani** sideboard is lacquered and has
extravagant gilded supports featuring lyres
and masks (*below*). c.1930 112in (284cm)
wide ★★★ ☆ ☆

A wrought-iron armature by **Louis Majorelle** provides a setting for a Daum Frères blown and cased pink glass vase with purple streaks. 1918–25 9.5in (24cm) high ★★★★★

A sandblasted pattern of stylized scallop shells decorates this vase designed by **Piero Fornasetti**. It was made by S.A.L.I.R., Murano. 1940 11.5in (29cm) high ★★★★★

A geometric pattern of overlapping stylized leaves decorates this vase, Malherbes by **René Lalique**. 1927 9in (23cm) high ★★★★★

The waterfall shape of these Sabino lampshades (*above*) was a popular motif for Art Deco designers. 1925 12.5in (31.5cm) ★★★★★

A brass table lamp with colorful shade designed by **Josef Frank** shows the positive delight in color and pattern in the Art Deco period (*right*). c.1925 17.75in (45cm) high ★★★★★

This early 1920s Schneider cameo glass bowl with scarab decoration is an excellent example of the fascination with Egypt (*above left*). The bowl is 10in (25.5cm) high ★★ ★ ★ ★ ★

Again by the Schneider glass house, this bowl (*above*) imitating marble employs the geometric decoration so favored by Art Deco artists. 1922–25 8.8in (22.3cm) high ★★ ★ ★ ★ ★

The artist Edgar Brandt is well known for his stylized metalwork. In this candlestick (*left*) he uses the motifs of the dove and fruit in contrast to the pitted, industrial metal. c.1925 16.25in (41cm) high ★★ ★ ★ ★ ★

Designed by **Carlo Scarpa** for the Muranese firm of Cappellin in 1930, this glass vase has a distinctly modern look (*below*). Scarpa uses the incamiciato technique—two superimposed layers, one of lattimo glass and one of colored transparent glass. 6.5in (17cm) high ★★★ ★ ★ ★

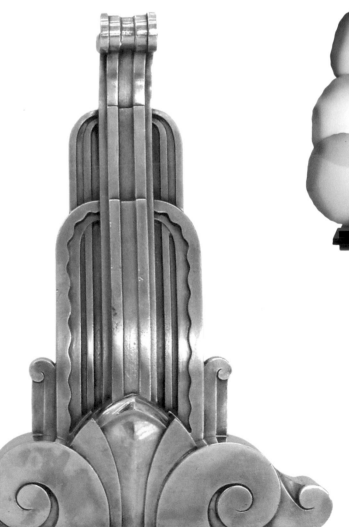

This early 1920s clock (*top*) employs Art Deco symbols to dramatic effect: the geometric shape, the two-toned onyx, the pentagon face with the fashionable numbers, and particularly the stylized antelope. 21in (54cm) wide ★ ★ ★ ★ ★ ★

With this pair of late 1920s table lamps, the contrast between the ebonized wood bases and the peach, amber, and white petals creates the illusion of fire (*above*). 8in (20.25cm) high ★ ★ ★ ★ ★ ★

This American andiron, which would always have been part of a pair, features the water fountain motif that was popularized during the 1925 Paris Exposition. This high Art Deco relief design was cast of solid, polished aluminum and bronze. 1930 20.25in (51.5cm) high ★ ★ ★ ★ ★ ★ the pair

Ercole Barovier

The Primavera series
1929–30

Ercole Barovier (1889–1974) was a member of one of Murano's oldest and most successful glassmaking families, active from the middle of the 13th century. He joined the family firm Vetreria Artistica Barovier & Co. in 1920, after initially studying medicine, and went on to become manager and head designer.

During his 50-year career he developed numerous decorative techniques and helped to bring about the 20th-century renaissance in Italian art glass. His first achievement was with the use of traditional murrine, but his most notable early creation was the Primavera range. The collection was launched at the 1930 Venice Biennale and included compotes, vases, and other vessels. However, the centerpiece was a bird made from blown glass that was considered to be so significant it was given a full-page illustration in the catalogue.

Primavera was an immediate and international success, no doubt owing to the unusual glass used, reminiscent of a cobweb suspended in colorless glass. Internally decorated with a white crackled netting, the glass was applied with bold blue or black sections. However, only a limited number of pieces were produced—only three of the iconic birds are known to exist—and as the chemical combination used to create the glass was the result of an accident the method proved impossible to reproduce. But it was not the last of Barovier's discoveries.

During the 1930s Barovier experimented with new multi-colored effects, most notably the process he called *colorazione a caldo senza fusion*, or "coloring [glass]while hot without fusing." He used this technique for many of his future designs, and it was adopted by other Muranese glassworkers.

In 1936 the Barovier glassworks merged with Fratelli Toso, and the new company was known as Barovier & Toso. Following World War II, Barovier began to reinterpret traditional glass forms. His glass combined colors and patterns including spirals, patchwork, stripes, squares, and circles. In the 1940s he used thick glass to create a series of organic, textured shapes such as the Lenti vase and the Oriente series, which featured trapped silver foil (and was re-issued in the 1970s).

In the 1950s Barovier's creations were defined by the use of "primitive" shapes, textured raw surfaces (such as in his Barbarici series), vivid colors, and complex patterns. The following decade saw him use unusual colors for tesserae glass, including the Intarsio series, for which he used thin triangles of glass to decorate a blown glass surface. They were then covered with clear glass and blown again to create a pattern of expanded triangles.

The clear, slightly milky glass that makes up the body of this Primavera vase contrasts with the solid black of the applied rim and handles. The vase was designed by **Ercole Barovier** for Vetreria Artistica Barovier & Co. This glass technique is extremely complicated. 1929–30 13.25in (33.5cm) high ★★★★★

Ercole Barovier's confidence as a designer can be seen in the bold stature of the Pigeon. It was shown at the 1930 Venice Biennale, an extremely early date for such a whimsical design. 1929–30 12in (30cm) high ★ ★ ★ ★ ★

Murano

During the 1920s and '30s a small group of glassmakers and designers turned their backs on the traditional, Renaissance-style glass being made by most of the factories in favor of modern designs. **Paolo Venini** was among the first to create revolutionary pieces. The company of which he was a partner, Venini & Co., went on to be Italy's leading post-war glassworks. He employed many forward-thinking designers, including **Napoleone Martinuzzi**, who developed a unique, sculptural style. He took the shapes of traditional vases and added decoration such as handles and rims. He also made animal sculptures and plant shapes and developed new materials including pulegoso ("bubbly") glass. From 1932 he worked with **Francesco Zecchin**, at the Zecchin-Martinuzzi Vetri Artistici e Mosaici, where he made opaque and pulegoso glass.

From 1934 to 1947 Venetian architect **Carlo Scarpa** worked as the artistic director of Venini & Co. He developed several decorative techniques seen as hallmarks of the factory's output. These include different types of cased glass including sommerso, where a transparent, colored core is enclosed by one or more differently colored transparent layers of glass and a transparent, colorless outer layer, and sommerso a bollicine, which features gold inclusions. He also created the iridescent corroso glass, with its distinctive matt surface; the textured battuto, which has a carved surface reminiscent of hammered metal; lattimo, an opaque milk-white glass; the spiraling striped mezza filigrana; tessuto, a fabriclike effect created by finely striped glass canes; the a bugne vase with its applied prunts or swirls; and the square occhi vase overlaid with a mosaic of murrines.

The Fratelli Toso factory also broke new ground. It was the first Murano factory to collaborate with an international artist, commissioning the German ceramicist **Hans Stoltenberg-Lerche** to create exhibition pieces from 1910 until 1914. His designs featured glass chips and metallic powders.

The Fratelli Barovier factory (known as Barovier & Toso from 1936) began to specialize in brilliantly colored and innovative new art glass under designer **Ercole Barovier**. By the 1930s factories were starting to use innovative forms and techniques that would be seen after World War II.

A subtly colored Barovier & Toso vase on a transparent French acrylic desk and a 1930s Murano clear glass chandelier add to the light, airy feel of this white room.

Geometric design enhances the colors of a vase by **Vittorio Zecchin** for Cappellin Venini & Co. c.1925 13.5in (34cm) high ★★★★★★

Square handles contrast with the round shape of **Vittorio Zecchin**'s vase, made by Venini & Co. c.1925 5.5in (13.8cm) high ★★★★★★

Applied handles enhance the textured glass used by **Napoleone Martinuzzi** for a pulegoso vase. c.1930 14in (36cm) high ★★★★★★

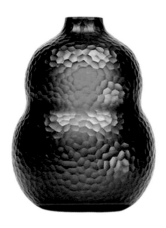

This battuto vase, designed by **Carlo Scarpa**, appears to have been beaten with a hammer. 1940 7.5in (17.5cm) high ★★★★★★

This corroso amphora, after a 1938 design by **Carlo Scarpa**, reinterprets a classic. c.1948 10.25in (26cm) high ★★★★★★

The surface of this Venini battuto vase by **Carlo Scarpa** has been carved to a textured finish. 1940 8in (20.5cm) high ★★★★★★

A red glass base is cased in clear glass decorated with bubbles for this Barovier vase. 11in (28cm) high ★★★★★★

Thick horizontal ribs create a bold, geometric silhouette for this vase designed by **Napoleone Martinuzzi** and made by Venini & Co. 1930 11.75in (29.5cm) high ★★★★★★

Decorative elements

The clean lines and luxurious materials used for Art Deco furnishings create sumptuous, elegant interiors. Many designers of the era used little in the way of surface decoration, letting the grain of the wood, texture of a fabric, or form of the piece they had designed become the ornamentation. Walls and floors are often best left plain or covered with textured or simple geometric patterns such as subtle stripes or parquet lozenges. These contrast with plain wooden surfaces or the graceful curves of French-influenced tables and chairs.

Art Deco rooms—whether they were dining, living, or bedrooms—often featured a suite of matching furniture. The effect can be re-created today, or choose pieces that complement each other for a more relaxed interpretation of the style.

These bold, simple rooms can be enhanced by allowing table legs, window frames, and window treatment such as wooden blinds to add further rectilinear elements.

Some Art Deco furniture was inspired by ancient Greek and Roman forms. These can be incorporated into a room by using sculpture or furniture based on such pieces. Other pieces were influenced by the new Modernist movement, and these can be used to add an accent feature among other Art Deco designs.

The bronze supports of this re-edition of an occasional table by **Jacques Adnet** create an architectural base for the circular oak top (*above right*). Adnet worked from the 1920s to the 1940s, and took a logical, refined approach, applying stark functionalism, yet he believed in subtle ornamentation and mixed modern design with traditional.

A table inspired by Cubism, and particularly by the Romanian sculptor **Constantin Brancusi**, provides an asymmetrical contrast to a **Josef Hoffmann**, Cube or Kubus armchair (*right*). The square quilting of the leather upholstery is typical of Hoffmann's geometric decoration. The chair was designed in 1910.

A bark-inspired printed canvas contrasts with oak paneling on the walls of this library (*opposite*). A **Gio Ponti** chair paired with a Jacques Adnet desk and **Curtis Jeré** lamp create a conversation corner. The classical marble head and 18th-century candlestick add historical perspective.

Having an 18th-century room with an ornate fireplace need not dictate the style (*above*). Good style will sit well with any period. The 1780s classical fireplace is balanced by the equally classical 1920s chair, designed by **Emile-Jacques Ruhlmann**.

The influence of Art Deco survived much longer than the period itself. The strong lines preferred by the Deco designers resonated through the 20th century and into the 21st. The striking, simple lines of this room make a perfect backdrop for the geometric lectern, the modern art, and the upholstered chair by Canadian furniture designer **Thomas Lamb**, who was inspired by a 1930s piece (*opposite*).

An **Alison Berger** crystal pendant chandelier brings a contemporary touch to a dining room furnished with a vintage mahogany table surrounded by 1920s **Jean-Michel Frank** tub chairs (*opposite*). The chocolate-brown Venetian plaster walls help to create a sumptuous period feel.

Art Deco interiors put an emphasis on luxury. A similar ambience has been created in this living room, which is furnished with a vintage console, parchment-covered armchairs, and tabourets by Jean-Michel Frank together with an **André Arbus** daybed and a 1940s French limestone table on a vintage rug by **Märta Måås-Fjetterström** (*above*).

INDUSTRIAL SKYSCRAPER

The French Art Deco style influenced furniture around the world, and in New York a handful of designers gave it a particularly American flavor. Names such as Norman Bel Geddes and Paul Frankl were inspired by the skyscrapers being built all over Manhattan to create furniture that reflected the city's new skyline. They used smooth contours, sleek and exotic woods, and new materials, such as chrome and plastics, to create furniture suitable for machine production; this was celebrated at the 1939 World's Fair. Motifs such as contrasting banding and asymmetrical geometric shapes used on the outside of buildings were repeated inside on vases, light fittings, and murals.

opposite, clockwise from top left A sheepskin covering softens the geometric, bent plywood form of the laminate daybed designed by **Marcel Breuer** for Isokon in 1925. / A pair of **Ludwig Mies van der Rohe**'s iconic Barcelona chairs bring an element of 20th-century design to an 18th-century-style room. The vertical and horizontal planes of the books behind them enhance their forms. / Almost all the furniture in the sitting and dining room of **Walter Gropius**'s Massachusetts house was designed by fellow Bauhaus designer Marcel Breuer. The room is a microcosm of the history of contemporary European design between 1920 and 1940. / Molding plywood was one of the industrial processes that became popular in the Art Deco period, influencing later designs. This Georgian wood paneling provides a perfect backdrop to the simple form of an **Eames** chair. The patina of the chair, paneling, and floorboards mellow the contrasts between the different elements.

right A Marcel Breuer chair and daybed are set against a backdrop of tall windows and floor-to-ceiling curtains. The modern effect is enhanced by a Tribal art sculpture.

The machine age

The 1920s and '30s were a time of progress, and this modernization can be seen in the streamlined furnishings predominately produced in America. This modern age began in 1918 with a burst of energy released in reaction to the horrors of World War I. The result was liberating and revolutionary.

Furniture echoed the geometric shapes of New York's emerging skyline—especially that cathedral to the motor car, the Chrysler Building—and speeding automobiles and trains. New industrial materials such as Bakelite and chrome found their way into homes in Europe and the U.S.

The Swiss-born French architect **Le Corbusier** (Charles-Edouard Jeanneret) wanted to create furniture as radical as his buildings. In 1927 he began working with **Charlotte Perriand** after seeing an exhibition of her anodized-aluminum and chromed-steel furniture. A year later the renowned Grand Confort range went on sale. It included the revolutionary B306 chaise longue—which still looks modern today—and the cube-shaped armchair that was based on a club chair, but with the tubular steel frame displayed on the outside rather than hidden underneath the upholstery.

In America, a form of Art Deco known as Art Moderne was inspired by the country's vibrant cities, which were home to towering skyscrapers and fashionable jazz bars. It came to the fore after the Wall Street Crash of 1929, when its focus on new technology and innovative materials began to influence architecture and interior design and offered to boost the ailing economy. The style gained international exposure through Hollywood movies such as 1932's *Grand Hotel*.

The earliest streamlined designs were for trains and ocean liners that featured contoured forms designed to decrease turbulence and reduce air resistance. The result was a glamorous new way to travel that celebrated speed, and a style of design that was copied for hotels, restaurants, stores, and gas stations.

Soon new homewares such as radios, vacuum cleaners, cookers, and refrigerators such as **Raymond Loewy**'s 1934 design for Sears were being made in this new style, and from new materials such as plastic, rubber, and vinyl. As well as representing new forms of technology, these items brought the new glamour into people's homes. Their unadorned surfaces were easy to mass-

Architecture doesn't come any more Art Deco than the Chrysler Building in New York. Its distinctive spire was inspired by the hub caps of Chrysler cars, and it celebrates both the Age of Speed and the motor car. It is the cathedral of Art Deco.

Tubular steel was the delight of designers of the 1920s and '30s. It was versatile, and strong and created statement pieces—none more than this daybed with its contrasting animal-hide seat.

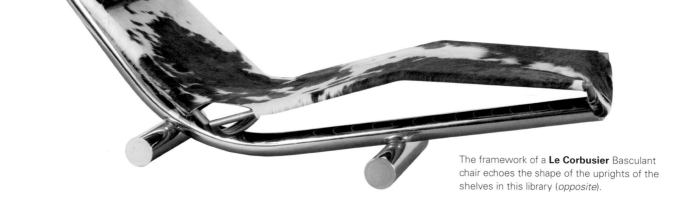

The framework of a **Le Corbusier** Basculant chair echoes the shape of the uprights of the shelves in this library (*opposite*).

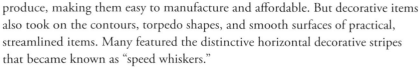

Edward Hald used the Graal technique to decorate this vase with stylized fish and pond weed (*above*). The reflections in the cased glass give the impression of more fish and fronds. This design was launched by Orrefors in 1937. 7.5in (18.5cm) high ★ ★ ★ ★ ★ ★

Graphic and geometric vintage pieces in stainless steel and Perspex set against shimmering gray wallpaper create a glamorous and elegant 1930s-style urban apartment (*opposite*).

The thick glass walls of this Steuben bowl are a sign of quality (*below*). The engraved Gazelle design by Sidney Waugh shows typically Art Deco stylization. The base is a quintessential 1930s form. 1935 7in (18cm) high ★ ★ ★ ★ ★ ★

produce, making them easy to manufacture and affordable. But decorative items also took on the contours, torpedo shapes, and smooth surfaces of practical, streamlined items. Many featured the distinctive horizontal decorative stripes that became known as "speed whiskers."

Some of the most eye-catching streamlined furniture was made by **Paul Frankl** and **Donald Deskey**, both based in New York. Frankl was born in Czechoslovakia; he trained as an architect and emigrated to the U.S. in 1914. On his arrival he became enamored with New York City and the possibilities it offered for "modern living." At first he worked as an architect and furniture designer, but by the mid-1920s he was concentrating on furnishings. His signature Skyscraper furniture—inspired by the high-rise buildings that already dominated the Manhattan skyline—was launched in 1926.

Deskey worked in many fields, including metal furniture, lighting, fabrics, wallpaper, and interiors. He often combined materials such as chromium, Bakelite, and aluminum, while sofas might feature black lacquer and rosewood highlighted with nickel-plated fittings. In his furniture he created a modern form that combined streamlining and the French Art Deco style.

A similarly dramatic evolution in style was seen in other forms of decoration. After World War I the French glass manufacturer Daum largely stopped making the cameo glass for which it was famed, and perfected an acid-etching technique. It used this to create monumental vases and lamps etched with geometric designs, some with a form of cameo outer layer and others overlaid with wrought-iron armature. Many studio glassmakers also used acid etching to create geometric patterns on glass. Among them was **Jean Luce**, who also decorated glass with hand-painted enamel patterns.

Designers brought a new style to cut glass. **Ludwig Kny**, who worked for Stuart & Sons, and **William Wilson** at Whitefriars (both in the U.K.) used bold geometric cutting on clear or pale glass, although traditional mid-19th-century forms were still made by the companies.

Abstract cut-glass designs were also created by Val Saint-Lambert in Belgium. These were more progressive than the factory's classic designs. Many pieces consist of one or two deeply colored layers of glass overlaid on to a clear body then cut with deep, repeating motifs.

A new and distinctive style of glass was made in Sweden. At Orrefors, designers **Simon Gate** (who was inspired by Neo-classical decoration) and **Edward Hald** (who used simple, elegant forms) championed engraved glass. Their elegant designs were named Swedish Grace when they were exhibited together at the 1925 Paris Exposition. At Kosta Boda, **Lars Kjellander** engraved figurative and naturalistic designs onto glass.

Artistic glassware was also made by Steuben in New York. Designer **Frederick Carder** created vases and tablewares in simulated hardstone colors known as Jade Glass. **Sidney Waugh** engraved the company's clear glass with figurative and geometric patterns.

In contrast, **Reuben Haley** at the Consolidated Lamp & Glass Co. of Coraopolis, Pennsylvania, transformed the two-dimensional principles of Cubist painting into its Ruba Rhombic range of vases and tablewares that were factory-produced and available at affordable prices.

This tile frieze by the innovative ceramicist **Frederick Rhead** was an inspiration to many of the Art Deco designers who followed.

Designed by New Zealander **Keith Murray** for Wedgwood in the 1930s, this ribbed vase was the height of modernity. Murray is rightly considered one of the most influential designers in the Art Deco style. 7.48in (19cm) high ★ ★ ★ ★ ★

The New Zealand architect **Keith Murray** also designed glass, but is best known for the Modern, geometric, monochrome-glazed pottery he designed for the British ceramics factory Wedgwood.

From 1924 to 1928 the Roseville factory in Zanesville, Ohio, created the geometric Futura ceramics line. The bowls usually have an architectural feel and are decorated with blended glaze colors, often combining pink with grey or blue.

The Fiesta range designed by **Frederick Rhead** for the Homer Laughlin China Co. of Newell, West Virginia, was introduced in 1936. The range's streamlined curves were an immediate hit with the public, and by its second year of production more than one million pieces had been produced.

The American company Cowan Pottery in Rocky River, near Cleveland, Ohio, produced an impressive range of decorative and functional ceramics (from vases to door handles), many in distinctive Art Deco styles. Notable pieces include pairs of pelican bookends by **A. Drexler Jacobson** and flower fogs (these were special flower holders designed to stand on water and hold cut blooms in position) by **Waylande Gregory**.

Metal decorative vases and tablewares also reflected this change of style, with established firms adding Modern, Art Deco designs to their ranges. By the 1920s Christofle was one of the largest metalworks of its kind in France, and added a comprehensive range of Art Deco designs to its catalogue in this period, from furniture mounts to cutlery services. Many of these pieces were designed by fashionable names such as **Maurice Dufrêne**, **André Groult**, **Paul Follot**, **Louis Sue**, **André Mare**, and **Gio Ponti**.

Another manufacturer that commissioned designers to make pieces in the new style was the Danish firm Georg Jensen. Possibly the most notable of these was **Johan Rohde**, who designed a sleek, naturalistic silver jug with an ebony-insert handle in 1920. It is still celebrated for its lack of applied decoration and the way in which the handle and lip appear to grow organically from the body of the vessel rather than be bolted on.

For many, the sense of freedom felt after World War I was expressed through drinking cocktails, and the silver, chrome and glass cocktail- and barware created during the 1920s and '30s evokes the spirit of the time—especially architectural cocktail shakers and novelty designs in the form of barmen or penguins.

Norman Bel Geddes designed sleek chrome pieces for the Revere Copper & Brass Co in Canton, Massachusetts, including the streamlined Manhattan drinks service and the Skyscraper cocktail shaker. He invented the term "industrial design," and opened the first industrial design studio in 1927.

Another factory that introduced an Art Deco range was the Chase Brass & Copper Co. of Waterbury, Connecticut. It produced affordable coffee sets, salt and pepper shakers, candlesticks, lamps, and cocktail shakers in a Modern style and made primarily from chrome and copper. Many of the successful ranges were designed by **Walter von Nessen** and **Russel Wright**.

The biomorphic form of this jug is typical of the work of **Henning Koppel**. He was inspired by the **Johan Rhode** pitcher designed in the 1920s. The satin surface of the silver pitcher—officially called 1052 but nicknamed The Swan—was developed by Danish firm Georg Jensen, for which he worked. 1956 16.5in (42cm) high ★ ★ ★ ★ ★ ★

A cocktail shaker was an essential part of a Jazz Age party. This late 1920s **Norman Bel Geddes** Ferris wheel-shaped chrome cocktail stand has glass accessories and two Manhattan chrome cocktail shakers. This was a "dress to impress" addition to the party. 24in (60cm) high ★ ★ ★ ★ ★ ★

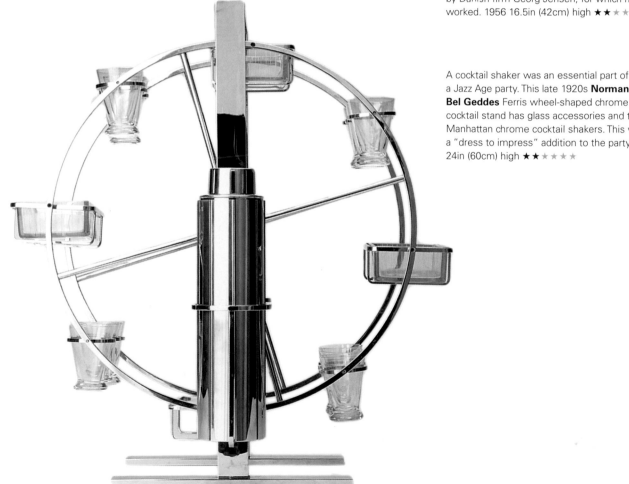

The Bauhaus

As a school of industrial design, the Bauhaus had a major influence on Modernist design, but its revolutionary ideas meant that it was never far from controversy. It was founded by **Walter Gropius** in Weimar, Germany, in 1919. He was a former pupil of the Modernist designer **Peter Behrens**, and used the school to further his involvement in the movement, with the aim of introducing unity in the arts and reassessing the fundamental purpose and nature of good design. The tutors he employed included **Wassily Kandinsky**, **Marcel Breuer**, **Paul Klee**, and **Laszlo Moholy-Nagy**. The results—including enamel and Bakelite desk lamps and cantilever chairs made from chrome-plated metal—were copied the world over.

Students at the Bauhaus began their training with a foundation course, after which they went on to specialize. They were taught to use new materials and focus on mass-production techniques. The school taught architecture, furniture, pottery, painting, weaving, graphic design, and stone-, metal-, and woodworking; students were encouraged to be confident working in as many of these disciplines as possible. Whether the students were designing ceramics, furniture, graphics, or textiles, product design was of the greatest importance.

Gropius and his fellow architects made use of advances in the use of steel and concrete to design buildings with few interior walls—they were no longer required for support—and which became known as the International Style. When the school moved to Dessau in 1925, Gropius designed the new building in the International style and was able to unify the school's objectives in the fields of art, craft and technology. Hannes Meyer took over as director in 1928, and the style of the Bauhaus's architecture became functional. He continued to focus on mass-produced design and removed parts of the curriculum that he believed were too formal. He also promoted the social function of architecture and design, believing the public good was more important than private luxury.

The Bauhaus building at Dessau—which was its home from 1925 until 1932—was built from concrete with glass curtain walls that were an innovation at the time.

The influence of the Bauhaus was immense, as was external influence on the school. **Le Corbusier, Charlotte Perriand,** and **Pierre Jean Jeanneret** collaborated on this LC-4 black leather and tubular steel chaise longue. 1928 64in (163cm) long ★★★★★

Lamps—desk lamps in particular—were the sort of practical design the Bauhaus excelled at. This example by **Marianne Brandt** and **Hin Bredendieck** has an enameled metal shade and Bakelite base. c.1928 17in (43cm) high ★★★★★

Thanks to Meyer's accurate costings of the buildings he designed, he was popular with prospective clients, and the school made its first profit in 1929. However, his firm communist views were not welcomed by the Nazi philosophy that was taking hold in the country. Meyer also alienated figures such as Breuer, who resigned. When he was replaced by **Ludwig Mies van der Rohe** in 1930 his supporters were banned from the school. Mies van der Rohe reorganized the curriculum again, giving it an increased emphasis on architecture. However, the Nazis continued to identify it as "un-German" and claimed it was a hotbed of Communism. As a result the school—which had moved to Berlin in 1932—closed in April 1933. But its legacy is undoubted thanks to its innovative designers, many of whom fled abroad to escape persecution under the Nazis.

For many, it is the furniture designs that were created at the Bauhaus that epitomize its work. Iconic pieces include Mies van der Rohe's cantilevered chairs and Breuer's B3 or Wassily chair, both of which are iconic machine-age designs. The B3 is a prime example of how Bauhaus designers created pieces for mass production. Breuer's prototype was welded together, but was developed into a nickel-plated frame with bolted joints. It was the first of a series of standardized, modular, tubular-steel furniture designed by Breuer that were functional, well-costed, and mass-produced. Other pieces that resonate today are the lamps designed by **Christian Dell**, **Marianne Brandt**'s teapots, and other tablewares, and **Anni Albers**' textiles.

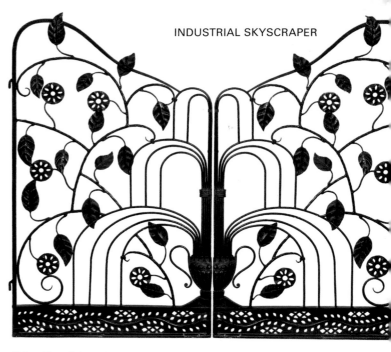

Edgar Brandt has taken a typical Art Nouveau image of a vase with flowers and leaves and given it a distinctly Art Deco stylized look. c.1924 52in (132cm) high ★★★ ☆ ☆

Marianne Brandt was the first woman to enroll in the metal workshop of the Bauhaus. This sculptural silver-plated brass and ebony teapot—model no. MT49—is such a famous design that it was featured on a German postage stamp. c.1927 6in (15cm) wide ★★★★★★

Ludwig Mies van der Rohe used a cane-work seat to contrast with the tubular steel frame of this MR-10 cantilevered chair. It was made by Josef Müller in Berlin. Late 1920s 32in (80cm) high ★★ ☆ ☆ ☆ ☆

Influential pieces

Stylized forms are the essence of many Art Deco pieces. Animals—particularly deer—were depicted in simple, bold formats that gave their natural beauty a modern elegance. The human body—primarily the female form—was also transformed into an idealized, sensual being with elongated limbs. Many figures are depicted in the middle of a dance, with their limbs outstretched and clothing swirling around them to enhance the effect. Some of these pieces celebrate the joys of the Jazz Age, and the new freedom being enjoyed by women at the time.

Geometric designs and industrial influences were also fashionable and could be used alone or combined with stylized figures. For example, traditional cut-glass decoration was used to create eye-catching pieces.

Stylized antelopes feature on this large ovoid vase designed by **Charles Catteau** for Boch Frères (*above*). The enamel is typically thickly applied to create a pattern in relief, and the glaze is also crackled. c.1930 14in (35.5cm) high ★★ ★ ★ ★ ★

Viktor Schreckengost's Jazz designs for Cowan encapsulate the excitement of the era. This plate features dancing and cocktails—essential Jazz Age pastimes (*right*). c.1929 11.25in (28.6cm) diameter ★★★ ★ ★ ★

These **Paul Kiss** lamps with wrought-iron central barrels and gilded details are statement pieces at the epicenter of Art Deco style. 1925 71.5in (181cm) high ★★★★ ★ ★

A Val Saint-Lambert vase, in cased red glass cut with geometric vertical bands and a section of horizontal step cutting. The rim has a silver band. 1930s 10in (25cm) high ★★ ☆ ☆ ☆ ☆

A **Karl Hagenauer** highly stylized figure of a Flamencotanzerin (flamenco dancer) in a sculptural pose (*right*). The cast-metal torso and legs are joined to a carved wooden dress. 1930 9.5in (24.5cm) high ★★ ☆ ☆ ☆ ☆

Typically stylized leaping antelopes in bronze and elegant curlicues form the supports for these bookends by **Raymond Stubbs** (*below*). 1925 8in (20.5cm) high ★★ ☆ ☆ ☆ ☆

Marcel Breuer designed some of the most famous and most produced tubular-steel-and-leather classics. They fit into any room and are immediately recognizable. The design goes back to Breuer's productive years in Berlin from 1928 until 1931 during which, after leaving the Bauhaus, he worked as an independent architect and interior designer.

A spring developed by automotive engineer **George Carwardine** in 1932 allows the jointed support of his Anglepoise lamp to remain in position. The lamp has remained in production ever since. 35.5in (90cm) high ★★★★★★ reissue, Tecta

This Bauhaus table lamp, designed by **Christian Dell**, rotates in all directions. The Bauhaus prided itself on practicality and functionality. 1920s 17in (43cm) high ★★★★★★

Not all the designers of objects produced in the Art Deco period are known. It is often less expensive to go for the unknown and buy because of the style. This chrome and black enameled-metal table lamp, with original shade and chroming, looks the part. 1930s 18in (46cm) high ★★★★★★

Paul Evans' early metalware was much inspired by the pared-down industrial look of Deco. This pewter pitcher with rosewood handle would look equally at home in the 1920s or '30s (*left*). c.1952 11in (28cm) high ★★★★★★

Taking tea was an institution in the 1920s and '30s, and companies like the Parisian firm of Christofle produced a wide array of fashionable accessories. This 1930s silver-plated circular design with burr amboyna-wood handles was popular. Tray 20in (51cm) long ★★★★★★

Many of the American designers embraced the chromium-and-steel "new-look" frame but also used padded upholstery for comfort. A good example is this Gliding Settee, by **Gilbert Rohde**, model H-35. c.1934 78.25in (199cm) long ★★ ★ ★ ★

Many of **Eileen Gray**'s designs were designed to be functional while displaying an unusual asymmetry. Her E-1027 adjustable glass-and-chrome table is no exception. This design was named after the summer house E1027, which Eileen Gray built for herself and her collaborator, **Jean Badovici**. The name was developed from their initials: E is for Eileen, 10 for Jean (J is the 10th letter of the alphabet), 2 for B(adovici) and 7 for G(ray). 1927 27–40in (69.5–102cm) high ★ ★ ★ ★ ★ modern

Eileen Gray developed the initial design for her adjustable F-1027 table for her sister, who enjoyed eating breakfast in bed. Here, the iconic Modernist design is used as an occasional table. It is complemented by a pair of **Charles** and **Ray Eames** Aluminum Group chairs. While the chairs were designed for indoor and outdoor domestic use, they are often used in offices today.

Gerrit Rietveld

Red/Blue chair 1923

Gerrit Rietveld was born in Utrecht in 1888. Apprenticed to his father, a joiner, at the age of 11, he set up his own furniture workshop in 1917, and in that year designed one of the most iconic chairs of the 20th century—one that not only encapsulated his personal approach to design and manufacturing, but also gave physical form to many theoretical aspects of Modernism.

The relatively simple geometric construction of Rietveld's chair—13 rectangular rails set at right angles to each other, supporting four rectangular boards for the seat, back, and armrests—was primarily driven by his desire to make something beautiful from inexpensive machine-made parts. Ingeniously but simply secured together by a series of overlapping doweled joints (known as "Cartesian nodes"), the chair was originally conceived in wood with a natural wood finish. However, in 1923 Rietveld decided to give it a painted finish, and it was at that point that it acquired its name: the Red/Blue.

This painted finish—red back, blue seat, and the supporting framework in black with yellow ends—was no superficial decoration: in 1919 Rietveld had become a member of the De Stijl ("The Style") movement that, since 1917, had been the "dynamic equilibrium" in fine art and design through abstraction and geometry. One manifestation of this was the use of rectangles in flat planes of primary colors and black and white. A leading exponent of De Stijl was the Dutch artist Piet Mondrian (1872–1944), and comparisons were soon drawn between his work and Rietveld's chair—the latter being described as a "3-D Mondrian painting." Indeed, Rietveld's first building (he also qualified as an architect in 1919)—the Rietveld Schröder House, built in Utrecht in 1924—featured a radical top floor incorporating sliding walls to create and change the living spaces that was also lauded as a 3-D realization of a Mondrian painting.

Although Reitveld parted company with the De Stijl movement in 1928, in favor of a more functional style of architecture—he was, for example, one of the first architects to experiment with prefabricated concrete slabs—his early focus on clarity through geometry if anything intensified, and was best encapsulated in his Zig-Zag chair of 1934. An asymmetric, vertical-horizontal composition of four rectangular wooden boards, its seemingly simple construction—it is in fact secured by complex dovetailing—was perhaps even more revolutionary and, in the complete absence of applied decoration, even more Modernist than its illustrious Red/Blue predecessor.

The machine aesthetic and the strict code of the De Stijl movement can be seen in **Gerrit Rietveld**'s Red/Blue chair. This painted solid beechwood and plywood example, made by Cassina, was created in the same way. 34in (86.5cm) high ★ ★ ★ ★ ★ modern

A Modernist interior echoes the different planes of the Red/Blue chair and allows the colored sections to make a statement.

The Gropius house

After he fled Nazi Germany in 1934 **Walter Gropius** moved to England and then the United States. There he built a family home in Lincoln, Massachusetts, that combined Bauhaus principles with traditional New England materials, such as brick, wood, and fieldstone. The combined sitting and dining room in particular epitomizes the Modern philosophy and goals to which he aspired. Tubular steel chairs and side tables by **Marcel Breuer** fill the room. Light for reading is supplied by the type of lamp designed by many Bauhaus students. The simple design of the tableware chimes with the movement's desire to create elegant, functional pieces that were easy to mass-produce.

Elsewhere, simple shelving and functional desks allowed the architect and designer to work efficiently. Other pieces of furniture include the plywood Long Chair designed by Breuer for Isokon and desk chairs by **Eero Saarinen**.

The north façade of the Gropius house was revolutionary at the time, with its flat roof, ribbon windows, and plate-glass and glass blocks (*below*). The spiral staircase was installed so that their then 12-year-old daughter could access her room in privacy.

This sitting and dining room in Gropius's house is a microcosm of the history of contemporary European design between 1920 and 1940 (*right*). Almost all the furniture was designed by **Marcel Breuer**. Other pieces include an **Eero Saarinen** Womb chair and a **Sori Yanagi** Butterfly footstool.

A wall made of ribbed-glass bricks divides the study from the dining area, shielding it from noise but allowing the room to be part of the general space (*above*).

The bedside table next to the tubular-framed daybed is designed to act as a night table or, during the day, to swing under the long table of which it is part, to act as a shelf *(right)*.

Industrial design on show

The tubular-steel and leather chairs designed by Modernist designers at the Bauhaus and elsewhere in early 20th-century Europe look at home in many settings. **Ludwig Mies van der Rohe**'s Barcelona chair, stool, and coffee table provide a Modernist counterpoint to a white-painted paneled room with stripped floorboards and slate fireplace. Alternatively, they can be combined with other furnishings for a bold, contemporary look. Placing them in the center of the room allows the viewer to appreciate their simple, elegant construction. They are ideal for the kind of open, free-flowing interiors that Meis van der Rohe planned for the buildings he designed.

The LC2 or Grand Confort club chairs designed by **Le Corbusier** add a touch of luxury to open-plan interiors while fulfilling the Modernist brief that designs should remove all ornament that was not related to the structure and construction of a piece.

A single example of **Marcel Breuer**'s B3 or Wassily chair positioned in the corner of a room can become almost sculptural. It also enables the viewer to appreciate how revolutionary the design was when it first appeared, in 1925: nine pieces of metal tube welded together give the appearance of a single length and create a frame strung with five strips of leather. When transplanted to a rustic setting such as a converted barn, such pieces create a contrast to the natural stone and wood of the building. Combined with simple accessories and in rooms with plenty of natural light, these chairs take center stage in a way their creators may never have anticipated.

The traditional architecture of this Paris apartment makes a pleasing counterpoint to the Mid-Century Modern furniture—including **Mies van der Rohe** Barcelona chairs and stools—ranged around the room. Integral bookshelves meld into the original architecture and display a collection of treasured books.

Room spaces in this 1960s house in Sarasota, Florida, are created by positioning pieces of furniture by **Marcel Breuer** and **Le Corbusier** (*opposite*). The ageless quality of these pieces designed in the 1920s ensures they look perfectly in place in a Mid-Century Modern interior.

The blocks of contrasting color created by the floors and walls of this bedroom are enhanced by a tubular-chrome-framed table by Marcel Breuer and a Barcelona chair by **Mies van der Rohe**. The low partition wall screens the bedroom from the void of the staircase and the kitchen below (*above*).

Ludwig Mies van der Rohe's Barcelona chairs complement a collection of 1950s glass and a modern rug by **Angela Adams** that has a 1960s inspiration (*left*). The room has a sharp 1960s palette of black, red, charcoal, and white, which is set off by a white background.

An Op Art-inspired silvered acrylic bubble screen creates an unusual backdrop for the Barcelona chairs. They were commissioned in cherry red to complement the color scheme of the living space in this New York apartment (*above*).

Marcel Breuer's B3 chair—also known as the Wassily chair—was
one of the first pieces of furniture to be made from tubular steel and
is said to have been inspired by the handlebars of his bicycle. The
original chair was upholstered with fabric slings, but later versions
use five strips of thick leather. Here, the chair is juxtaposed with a
contemporary sculpture in front of a large picture window (*above*).

Furniture designed in the 1920s or '30s is nothing if not versatile.
While it is typically used in 20th-century buildings, here a converted
barn constructed from plywood, concrete and cement provides
an exceptional space. While the large, industrial building has been
modernized to contemporary standards, it still displays much of its
original construction, especially in the imposing beams (*opposite*).

SOFT MODERNISM

Warm, natural, and human are qualities rarely attributed to the Modern movement. But for designers working in what has become known as Soft Modernism, they were all-important. Rather than hard metal surfaces they used natural wood and fabrics to create interiors filled with modern, curving, organic designs. Like their Modernist colleagues they eschewed unnecessary ornamentation to create functional pieces ideal for open-plan living. Designs also celebrated tradition, craftsmanship, and attention to detail rather than the latest manufacturing techniques. The result was warm, informal interiors that were no less revolutionary than their Modernist counterparts.

opposite, clockwise from top left Deep leather cushions visually relieve the angles of the square wooden frame of this sofa and add to the comfort of the sitter. The use of these natural materials brings a human touch to a simple design. / The Finnish architect and designer **Alvar Aalto**'s rejection of steel and glass in favor of warmer, organic alternatives—particularly wood, as in this classic Aalto dining table and cantilevered chairs—led the way in softening and "humanizing" Modernism for the mid-20th century. / Although the Italian designer **Joe Colombo** eschewed wood in favor of hard steel and man-made, fiberglass-reinforced plastics for the structurally supportive elements of his furniture designs, overtly comfortable upholstery—evidenced here in his Elda armchair and his Roll sofa—softened them for both the sitter and the onlooker. / A wooden chest by **George Nelson**, one of the founders of American Modernism, sits beneath artwork by Jo Shane, and plays host to a small collection of family heirloom and flea-market-find glass and pottery that many early Modernists would have rejected as superfluous to function.

right An unattributed plain and overtly functional white seat raised on turned and splayed legs is softened in both appearance and use by the inclusion of a curved, low-profile, neutral-colored bentwood and hooped cane backrest.

A rounded alternative

The design style referred to as "soft modernism" began in Scandinavia in the 1930s as a reaction against the metal furniture being created in the rest of Europe. **Alvar Aalto** and **Bruno Mathsson** were at the forefront of the movement. They used wood—which was abundant in the region—to make gently curving, ergonomic and organic pieces that were inspired by nature.

Aalto, a Finnish architect, believed that metal furniture was uncomfortable in a cold climate and "unsatisfactory from a human point of view." His work emphasized traditional craftsmanship rather than the latest manufacturing techniques. Working with his wife, Aino, he used bent birchwood, which he discovered had similar properties to steel. His groundbreaking designs include the Tank armchair—the first cantilevered design to be made from wood. Other notable designs include the Paimio No. 41, a chair with a seat and back made from a single sheet of plywood. It was designed in 1931 for the Paimio tuberculosis sanatorium.

Aalto also designed glassware, including his 1936 Savoy vase for the Karhula-Iittala glassworks. Its flared, undulating shape was based on Finnish peasant dress and such was its success that it is still made today.

Marcel Breuer was one of the first to design a cantilevered chair using tubular steel, while he was at the Bauhaus in Germany. When he settled in England in 1935 he, too, turned to the softer appeal of molded plywood. The Long Chair he created for the Isokon Furniture Company was designed to be suitable for mass production and was based on an aluminum lounge chair he had designed two years earlier.

The Austrian-born architect and designer **Josef Frank** began his career as a leading figure in Viennese Modernism. But by the early 1920s he no longer agreed with the French architect **Le Corbusier**'s belief that a house should be a "machine for living in." Instead, he chose to work in a more artistic style that emphasized comfort and color. He designed furniture that could be "seen through"; for example, the legs of cupboards were long enough for people to be able to see the point where the wall joined the floor behind, and chairs had open backs.

Frank moved to Sweden in 1933, where he continued to design buildings, furniture, fabrics, wallpapers, and carpets. He also rejected the monochrome interiors advocated by other designers at the time. He wrote: "The monochromatic surface appears uneasy, while patterns are calming, and the observer is unwillingly influenced by the slow, calm way it is

The Austrian-born architect and designer **Josef Frank** co-founded the Vienna Werkbund in 1932, prior to emigrating to Sweden in 1933, where he went on to become the most prestigious designer in the Stockholm company Svenskt Tenn. It was for Svenskt that he designed, in 1939, this 966 mahogany armchair with a horseshoe-shaped backrest with flared supports, similar legs, and leather-covered upholstery.

The Modernist design of this model no. 98 Finmar tea trolley by **Alvar Aalto** features a linoleum top, natural birch frame, and lacquered wheels with rubber tread. It was every fashionista's dream. 1936–37 34.5in (88cm) wide ★ ★ ☆ ☆ ☆ ☆

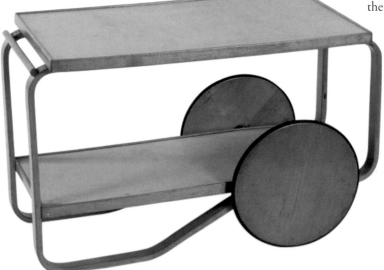

When painted coral pink, the plywood daybed **Marcel Breuer** designed for Isokon in 1925 provides a dramatic contrast to the green and black color scheme of this living room (*opposite*). The coral pink standard lamp also dates from the 1920s.

produced. The richness of decoration cannot be fathomed so quickly, in contrast to the monochromatic surface which doesn't invite any further interest and therefore one is immediately finished with it."

The trend for wooden rather than metal furniture was followed elsewhere in Europe. In the U.K., designers who had created pieces in the Arts and Crafts style began to make more modern pieces with an Art Deco look. Among those who created these hybrid designs were **Betty Joel**, who used curvilinear geometric shapes and exotic woods; **Harry** and **Lou Epstein**, who created dining suites using pale woods; and **Ambrose Heal**, who made modern pieces for his family's famous London store that offered a relatively affordable alternative to the plethora of antique-inspired pieces being sold elsewhere.

At the time the Dutch architect and furniture designer **Hein Stolle** was also looking for ways to use new materials to create affordable, mass-produced furniture. He used a single piece of bent plywood for a magazine table and the T46 coffee table he designed for Isokon in 1946 (it did not go into production until 2001), and a combination of molded plywood and a wooden frame for dining chairs in the 1940s.

In New York, **Gilbert Rohde** experimented with industrial materials such as Plexiglas, Lucite, and Bakelite, but also used wood for many of his modular furniture designs. He wanted to make modern design America's national style by designing affordable furniture suitable for mass production.

Finnish-born architect **Eliel Saarinen** settled in the United States in 1922. As well as designing furniture he was director of the Cranbrook Academy of Art in Bloomfield Hills, Michigan, and from where a modern, American style emerged. His students included **Harry Bertoia**, **Charles Eames**, **Florence Knoll**, and his son **Eero Saarinen**. His philosophy was: "Always design a thing by considering it in its next larger context—a chair in a room, a room in a house, a house in an environment, an environment in a city plan."

Soft modernism continued to be popular after World War II when consumers looked for comfort rather than novelty and designers such as Charles and **Ray Eames** were able to use new materials which had previously been available only for military purposes to produce good design available to all.

This very masculine upright chair with strong lines was designed in the 1920s by De Coene Frères. The leather upholstery and black lacquer frame with nickel feet was the height of French classical style.

Saarinen House on the Cranbrook Academy of Art campus in Michigan was designed by Finland-born architect **Eliel Saarinen** (father of Eero Saarinen) in 1928, and completed in 1930. Its restored dining room is an opulent, stylish, and comfortable example of how in the Modernist era Art Deco interiors could be eminently functional and overtly decorative without either of these desirable qualities being achieved to the detriment of the other (*opposite*).

Influential pieces

Furniture designers working in the Soft Modern style used local timbers such as birch and pine, although exotic woods such as mahogany might be used as a veneer. Chairs might feature innovative shapes created from bent plywood, or updates of traditional shapes. New materials such as chrome-plated metal tubes and glass were also used, but in a less minimal way than was seen in the work of Modernist designers. Cabinets were functional and generally featured minimal carving or inlays, as these designers preferred to let the grain of the wood provide the decoration. Occasionally veneers were used to create fashionable Art Deco decorations such as cross-hatched geometric patterns and sunbursts. Handles might be discreetly carved from the same wood as the body, or consist of simple metal designs. Legs and feet varied from simple blocks to elegant outswept shapes. Forms were often symmetrical and designed as part of a larger suite.

This classic octagonal walnut-framed chair was part of a table and six chairs designed by **Harry** and **Lou Epstein** in 1935 (*above*). These were the height of fashion for the more affluent young, and can still be found today. Chair 36in (92cm) high
★★ ☆ ☆ ☆ ☆ the set

Furniture designed by **Gilbert Rohde** combined the simplicity of Bauhaus design with a sense of form and ornamentation taken from Art Deco. This Art Deco lounge chair for Heywood-Wakefield Co. is one of a male and female pair (*left*). This is the female chair. c.1934 22.5in (57cm) wide ★★ ☆ ☆ ☆ ☆

Gerald Summers used a single sheet of cut and bent birch plywood to make this innovative, curved armchair for Makers of Simple furniture (*above left*). 1930s 23.75in (60.5cm) wide ★★★ ★ ★

An elegant bentwood frame contrasts with the rectilinear uprights of this easy chair designed by **Josef Frank** for Thonet Bros, Vienna (*above*). The wood has been stained brown. 1929 36in (90cm) high ★★ ★ ★ ★

Sweeping armrests contrast with the square back of this Swedish Art Deco chair (*left*). A further contrast is created by the pale birch frame and black leather upholstery. c.1930 25.25in (64cm) high ★★ ★ ★ ★

Geometric forms dominated **Betty Joel**'s work in the 1930s. This pair of Art Deco Queensland "silky oak" bedside cabinets has chrome disc handles (*right*). They were made by the Token Workers and retailed by J. C. Penney. 1934 36in (92cm) high ★ ★ ☆ ☆ ☆ ☆

Gio Ponti's furniture is characterized by elegant shapes and fine craftsmanship. This six-door sideboard with tapering legs has applied latticework to the doors (*below*). It was from an apartment building designed by Gio Ponti on Via Goldoni in Milan, Italy, pictured in the July 1938 issue of *DOMUS* magazine. c.1938 98.5in (250cm) wide ★ ★ ★ ★ ☆ ☆

These three-drawer birch chests, with rectangular birch handles and typical arched legs, are examples of **Alvar Aalto**'s early work (*above right*). c.1933 36in (91cm) wide
★★ ★ ★ ★ ★

Geometric cross-hatched mahogany parquetry covers the front of this elegant chest, designed by **Eugene Schoen** for Schmieg, Hungate and Kotzian (*above*). c.1935 45in (114.5cm) wide ★★★ ★ ★ ★

Birch veneers have been used to create an Art Deco starburst pattern on the front of this Swedish Art Deco sideboard (*right*). Ebony and mahogany create a marquetry motif in the center of each panel. c.1930 59in (150cm) wide ★★ ★ ★ ★

Alvar Aalto

The Tank 1936

Architect, designer, sculptor and painter **Alvar Aalto** was born in 1898. During his prolific career—he died in 1976—it is estimated that he designed over 500 industrial, civic, and residential buildings, mostly in his native Finland, but also in Italy, France, Germany, and the United States. While his earlier works were conceived in the Nordic Classical style, during the 1930s he embraced the International Modern style—but developed an innovative and ultimately highly influential approach to it. Underpinning this was his view that while the "machine age" concrete, steel, and glass forms of Modernists such as **Ludwig Mies van der Rohe** were quite rightly conceived to follow function, they were, nevertheless, deficient in what Aalto referred to as "human qualities."

Aalto's primary solution to this problem was to integrate an overtly organic material into his designs, and being a Finn that had to be wood—a material found in abundance throughout most of Scandinavia and prevalent in traditional Scandinavian architecture. However, the manner in which Aalto used wood was often far from traditional. Indeed, his groundbreaking research, in conjunction with his wife, Aino Marsio, and the carpenter-craftsman Otto Korhonen, into bending and molding laminated woods and plywood enabled him to deploy the material in revolutionary structural and aesthetic ways.

While prevalent in much of his architecture, Aalto's "humanizing" of Modernism is even more readily evident in his furniture and, especially, his now-iconic chair designs: No. 31 and No. 42, originally designed for the Paimio tuberculosis sanatorium in Finland, and also known as the Paimio chairs; and No. 400, originally designed for the 1936 Milan Triennale, and better known as the Tank because of its resemblance in profile to a World War I battle tank. Inspired by the cantilevered tubular-steel chairs developed by the Dutch architect **Mart Stam**, Mies van der Rohe and the Hungarian architect **Marcel Breuer** during the 1920s, Aalto's three chairs achieved the hitherto technically impossible: they employed warm wood rather than cold tubular steel for the combined arms-and-legs cantilevered frames. Aalto obtained the considerable strength and flexibility required of the material by using his revolutionary molded and laminated birchwood. Promoting good posture and supremely comfortable, they not only softened and humanized Modernism, but were also to provide important sources of inspiration for the post–World War II innovations of the American designers **Charles** and **Ray Eames**, and the Finnish architect **Eero Saarinen**.

Bent laminated birch was used to form the sides of **Alvar Aalto**'s Tank lounge chair, manufactured by Artek. This example has black velvet upholstery. c.1950 31in (79cm) high ★★★★★ for this date

The natural wood of Alvar Aalto's three-legged 90C tables and a Tank chair upholstered in a natural fabric complement the marble fireplace, white walls, and wooden wall-hanging in this living room.

The home of Alvar Aalto

Alvar Aalto's interiors show the organic nature of his furnishings and architecture and his desire to bring comfort and happiness to people. He treated each building he designed as a complete work of art—from the roof to the furniture and light fittings. The result was a human form of Modernism that was in harmony with the Finnish landscape. He made considerable use of timber and introduced plenty of natural light into his buildings.

The house Aalto designed with his wife, **Aino Marsio**, was furnished with their designs, which included bent plywood chairs, stools, tables, and trolleys. His furniture-making techniques were so successful that the couple set up their own company—Artek—to mass-produce them.

The use of wood—particularly Scandinavian birch—was important to Aalto. He once said: "The tubular steel chair is surely rational from technical and constructive points of view. It is light, suitable for mass production, and so on. But steel and chromium surfaces are not satisfactory from the human point of view."

The 406 armchair was designed in 1939 by **Alvar Aalto** (*above right*). The seat and back are made from woven linen tape suspended from the birch frame. The airy design is complemented in this setting by the Japanese bamboo screen behind it.

Alvar Aalto's tea trolley provides an unusual and moveable display space for houseplants (*right*). Bringing plants into the home adds to the soft, Modernist design of the room.

Aalto created a Modern version of the traditional Scandinavian hearth in the Villa Mairea, the home he designed for Harry and Maire Gullichsen in Noormarkku, Finland (*opposite*). The room is furnished with his designs as well as comfortable sofas to create a welcoming, functional room.

A simple table surrounded by birch chairs creates a comfortable yet practical dining space (*below*). Simple white shelves hold a collection of colorful vases and bowls while a traditional Scandinavian painted long-case clock provides a contrast in styles.

Sliding floor-to-ceiling doors create a flexible living space. Here they divide a children's playroom and provide an area to display the young artists' work (*right*). Child-sized versions of **Alvar Aalto**'s furniture add to the practical nature of the home.

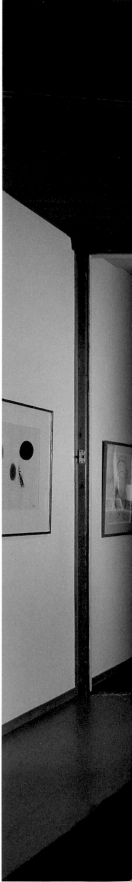

NEW LOOK

1946–1969

In tune with the new mood of optimism, designers explored new materials and techniques to create affordable, mass-produced furnishings.

George Nelson is famous for several iconic Mid-Century wall clocks. This pleated wooden wall clock has red and white enameled-metal hands and white pin numeral markers. c.1950s 3.15in (8cm) diam. ★★ ☆ ☆ ☆ ☆

Post-War Design Revolution

The end of World War II brought peace and optimism as well as a desire for comfort and reassurance. As prosperity returned, the demand for consumer goods grew—fueled in part by a housing boom. Traditional materials such as wood and fabric were combined with new ones such as molded fiberglass and plywood, developed for military purposes. Many revolutionary new forms were designed for mass production, and affordable for many. The 1950s and '60s saw a growth in youth culture that brought with it a new, affluent clientele, and new experiences such as foreign travel. Advances in science, and the space race, also influenced design, from lampshades to fabric.

A sleek **George Nelson** Bubble ceiling light, with bulbous ribbed shade, brought a look of the Space Age into the home. It was designed in 1955. 20in (51cm) high ★ ★ ★ ★ ★ ★

A 1950s **Charles Eames** for Herman Miller fiberglass-shell low armchair in orange on a black cat's cradle base was the height of modernity. 24.25in (61.5cm) high ★ ★ ★ ★ ★ ★

A 1950s Royal Copenhagen faience vase, no. 139/2878, designed by **Inge Lise Sørensen** and **Mariann Johansen**. This is known as the Surreal series, owing to its unusual motifs. 7in (17.75cm) hgih ★ ★ ★ ★ ★ ★

The **Le Corbusier** chaise longue, spaceship lamp, and Art Deco skiing poster bring a 20th-century feel to this 18th-century living room (*opposite*).

As design classics, many Knoll designs are still in production (*above*). If you want the look but don't want to pay for the original, many sites offer reproductions. It may not be the best investment, but it is a way of getting a vintage look without paying a vintage price.

The impact of World War II on the decorative arts was both adverse and considerable. Numerous materials and manufacturing facilities were diverted from arts and crafts to sustain the war effort, while the privations and austerity that stemmed from the conflict meant most people could not afford to buy decorative artifacts or indulge in interior design. The economic revival necessary to turn this around began in the country that had suffered neither invasion nor bombing, and which also had the largest economy: the United States. A remarkably rapid post-war return to beyond pre-war productivity levels there meant that by 1948, via the Marshall Plan, the United States was able to inject the equivalent of $100 billion in today's money into the various European economies, with the result that by 1951 most of those had also revived to pre-war levels and beyond.

With the financial ability both to manufacture and consume significantly restored, the core issue for the decorative arts was now one of style, and one of the first overt post-war indications of the direction things were heading in emerged on the catwalks of haute couture—specifically, in the French designer Christian Dior's Spring–Summer Collection of 1947. Tagged by *Harper's Bazaar* as the "New Look," it featured extravagant use of fabric and a revival of a curvaceous, feminine look that was not only in marked contrast to the flatter, more rectilinear styles of the late 1920s and the '30s, but was also a glamorous antidote to wartime austerity. This was a stylistic reaction that had been gradually fermenting elsewhere in the decorative arts.

The new style that developed after the war, dominating the 1950s and enduring into the early 1960s, has become known as Mid-Century Modern. In fact, there had already been an inkling of it in embryonic form as early as the 1930s, a decade in which some Scandinavian designers had developed a distinctive, curvaceous style of furniture known as Soft Modernism (see pages 88–103). While adhering to the basic simplicity of line and form of Modernist furniture, these designers had rejected the coldness of the mass-produced materials such as steel and plastic from which much of it was made. The solution of **Alvar Aalto** and other Scandinavian designers such as **Bruno Mathsson**, was to use natural materials—most notably wood—in less machinelike and more organic and sculptural forms. They combined functionalism with Swedish craft tradition.

The Scandinavian promotion of wood in this context was, in the early 1940s and on the other side of the Atlantic, embraced and developed by the American designers **Charles** and **Ray Eames**. They developed a method for molding bonded plywood in more than one direction. This technique, when adapted to industrial production, allowed the Eameses to create a host of innovative furniture designs after the war and throughout the 1950s that brought good design to a wider market. Developments during the war also allowed new materials to be brought into the field of design for homes. Throughout the war military designers, especially in the aircraft industry, had pioneered a number of new materials and techniques that were to give the decorative arts designers of the 1950s much greater freedom than had hitherto been possible. For example, very lightweight but relatively strong and durable aluminum featured increasingly in furniture construction, as did thinner and lighter steel—the latter inspiring the creation of lightweight wire-rod furniture by designers such as **Harry Bertoia** and **Warren Platner**.

Other new materials that were to have a profound effect, especially in furniture design, included new forms of upholstery. Notable among these were a type of rubber padding developed by tire manufacturers in Italy and, from Scandinavia, foam padding made from polystyrene beads that could be steamed into just about any shape that was desired. When this padding was applied over an almost equally moldable fiberglass frame, it became possible to produce very curvaceous, streamlined, and sculptural-like forms, such as Danish designer **Arne Jacobsen**'s Swan and Egg chairs.

Perhaps the biggest development in new materials and techniques, however, derived from the greater affordability of petroleum-based plastics as a result of an oil glut during the 1950s and '60s. Combined with new injection-molding techniques, designers were able fully to exploit plastic's ability to retain almost any form and, just as significantly, take advantage of the fact that it could produced in a veritable kaleidoscope of colors.

In addition to making much greater use of color, and creating more curvaceous, sculptural forms than their Modernist predecessors, the Mid-Century Modernists also revived, to varying degrees, the use of decorative pattern. Many of the patterns that became fashionable were, like the curvaceous sculptural shapes they employed, inspired by nature. One important difference, however, was that many of the natural shapes employed in the mid-20th century had never been seen prior to the development of very powerful electron microscopes. Of these newly discovered microscopic forms—there were many, including the surprisingly symmetrical crystalline composition of snowflakes—the asymmetrical amoeba provided the greatest source of inspiration. Amoeboid motifs became particularly prevalent in patterns applied to wallpaper, furnishing fabrics, ceramics, and glass.

Sometimes referred to as "Organic Modernism," this new microscopic natural imagery had been the product of a technological development, and in that respect had its counterpart in the Space Age imagery—notably table lamps in the form of rockets and ceiling pendants in the shape of flying saucers—that also proved popular from the late 1950s, as the technological push to put man into space gathered momentum and increasingly captured the public imagination.

Russel Wright was an industrial designer, and in 1936 he designed the American Modern dinner service for

A **Harry Bertoia** for Knoll Diamond chrome wire chair seems to float in air (*opposite bottom*). It was designed in 1953. 30in (76.25cm) high ★ ★ ★ ★ ★

Originally designed in 1958 for the Radisson SAS Hotel in Copenhagen, **Arne Jacobsen**'s Swan chair, which was manufactured by Fritz Hansen, Denmark, was an overnight sensation (*below*). The Swan sofa is still in production. 30.25in (77cm) high ★ ★ ★ ★ ★ ★

A sitting area in the Villa Mairea, a rural retreat in Noormarkku, Finland, commissioned by Harry and Maire Guillechsen, designed by **Alvar Aalto**, and built in 1938–39. For a Modernist architect, this particular space within the house is a relatively relaxed interior, but as such, especially in its deployment of a traditional hearth and use of brick, stone, and, above all, wood, it does much to explain why Aalto is seen as pioneering the "humanization" of Modernism.

Steubenville in Ohio. (It has become the most widely sold American dinnerware in history.) He turned away from the familiar geometric Art Deco style and was instead inspired by natural, organic forms. His practical and affordable products brought the Mid-Century Modern style into a vast number of American homes throughout the 1940s and '50s.

Following the widespread trauma of World War II, the public at large in most countries really did appear to want a "new look." Reinforcing this desire was a post-war growth in communications. Events such as the Festival of Britain in 1951 and the Good Design Exhibition in New York the previous year promoted the new designs and products of the Mid-Century Modernists in a traditional manner. However, combined with advertising (both direct and in the form of product placement), the new medium of television began to bring the prospect of these exciting new products right into people's homes. Moreover, as the post-war population, and with it suburbia, boomed, the sheer volume of demand for enticing new and well-designed furnishings, tableware, and all manner of kitchen and utility-room appliances mushroomed.

Although the Festival of Britain was centered in London, travelling satellite exhibitions were set up in other parts of the country. This is an exterior view, taken in April 1951, of the exhibition at the City Hall in Manchester (*below*).

The cover of an official guide for the 1951 Festival of Britain (*above*), a showcase of the best of British art, design, and industry.

NATURAL ORGANIC

Advances in technology and materials allowed designers to create organic shapes from plywood and tubular steel. These materials—which had previously been used to make rigid, geometric forms—produced softer shapes for furniture that combined comfort and function. The thinner, lighter tubular steel and strong plywood meant that tables and chairs were slimmer and pared down, but just as robust as their predecessors. Another breakthrough was that designers were able to make single-component furniture, such as a chair with a back and seat molded from one sheet of wood. As well as being attractive, these objects were easy to mass produce, and affordable.

opposite, clockwise from top left Although **Charles** and **Ray Eames**'s 1956 lounge chair with matching ottoman is a technically sophisticated piece of man-made engineering, it also has a substantial organic component: in its curved plywood, rosewood-veneered shell and its leather-covered upholstery. This gives it what Charles Eames wanted: "the warm receptive look of a well-used first baseman's mitt." / Organic material—teak—is echoed in an organic form—a teardrop—in this two-tier Mid-Century Modern coffee table. / A row of Charles and Ray Eames's classic DCWs (Dining Chairs Wood): conceived in 1945–46 and constructed from bent plywood, their comfortable seats and back were, in their softly undulating and rounded shape, inspired by the gentle curves of the humble potato crisp. / In a New York loft, the rigidly geometric forms of a 20th-century daybed, inspired by Classical and Neo-classical prototypes, is counterbalanced by the more curvaceous, organic qualities of a simple wooden table and a **Poul Kjærholm**-esque chair.

right The inherently warm tones of polished Brazilian hardwoods, woven grass paneling and vegetable-dyed woolen rugs balance the cooler white and off-white palette of the architectural shell in a bedroom in interior designer Hubert Zandberg's Berlin apartment.

Hans Wegner wishbone chairs, designed in 1949, are probably his most celebrated work. They are a triumph of craftsmanship with a simple design and clean lines that fit into any home. Here they are paired with a vintage zinc table and modern brightly colored molded-plastic chairs.

Design goes global

The demand for the elegant, comfortable and simple furniture being designed in Scandinavia and North America influenced furniture designers around the world. In Brazil—notably in Rio de Janeiro—furniture-makers including **José Zanine Caldas**, **Joaquim Tenreiro**, and **Sergio Rodrigues** handmade pieces using local hardwoods and upholstered with leather. Tenreiro, considered to be the father of 20th-century Brazilian furniture design, is known for his attention to detail, with curves and hand-carved details often hidden under seats. Rodrigues combined Classical details, contemporary shapes, and traditional woodworking skills to make elegant, sensual furniture. His best-known piece is the Poltrona Molé or "soft armchair," on which thick leather upholstery is draped over a solid, cylindrical wooden frame. In contrast to them, Caldas began making plywood furniture but later carved organic, sculptural pieces from huge logs.

Japan, too, developed a new aesthetic, but its designers made modern pieces based on vernacular furniture and using traditional techniques. **Isamu Kenmochi** visited Europe and the United States during the 1940s and '50s, and on his return was inspired to make traditional Japanese furniture that owes a debt to the contemporary furniture he had seen abroad.

One of the most successful Japanese designs of the period was the Butterfly stool by **Sori Yanagi**. Made from two sheets of laminated and molded beechwood and joined by a single stretcher, the seat resembles a butterfly in flight. It is said to have been inspired by a Japanese pictograph.

The Danish designer **Finn Juhl** fueled the international appetite for the Scandinavian aesthetic that helped to inspire this sculptural furniture when he won five gold medals for his exhibits at Milan Triennale shows during the 1950s. His Chieftains chair has an exposed teak frame, and the leather-upholstered back and seat appear to be suspended in mid-air. The furniture of fellow Dane **Poul Kjærholm** has similar sculptural qualities, but he also took advantage of the development of thin steel rods to bring subtle metal elements to his designs.

The Danish architect **Poul Henningsen** was fascinated with light and its importance to human life. He dedicated himself to creating soft, diffused interior lighting, and designed a series of different layered shades, such as the brushed copper leaves of his famous Artichoke lamp.

Other designers concentrated on making spare, sculptural furniture. **Hans Wegner**'s timeless JH501 chair features a seamless teak frame with a woven seat. Some say it is the ultimate blend of form and function.

In Italy **Gio Ponti** achieved the same simplicity with pieces such as his Superleggera ("super light") chair, which was based on a simple country chair and was the lightest chair in the world at the time.

In a different interpretation of the new style, the Italian **Carlo Mollino** took the elegant upholstered pieces of designers such as Finn Juhl and **Eero Saarinen** and the molded plywood used by **Charles** and **Ray Eames** and transformed them into bold, sensual, organic furniture in a style known as Turinese Baroque.

Wendell Castle is often acknowledged as the father of the American craft furniture movement. He studied art and industrial design at the University of Kansas and made his first piece of furniture as a graduate student in sculpture. He

The blocklike simplicity of this three-part caviona-wood credenza designed by the Brazilian **Joaquim Tenreiro** in the 1950s highlights the wood's patina and distinctive grain (*above*). 147in (373.5cm) long NPA

A 1950s marine-wood coffee table designed by the Brazilian **José Zanine Caldas** has a sculptural quality. 27.5in (70cm) deep NPA

The Kashiwado chair was designed by **Isamu Kenmochi** in 1961. Blocks of cedar trunk form this dynamic chair, named after a famous sumo wrestler. 25in (63cm) high ★★★★★

The **Sori Yanagi** rosewood Butterfly stool was designed in 1954. The stool is unmistakably modern while displaying a distinctively Japanese sensibility. 17.5in (44cm) high ★★★★★

In a minimal open space the eye is drawn to a simple table and an unusual chair (*opposite*). One of the mid-20th century's most striking examples of molded plywood, **Norman Cherner**'s wasp-waisted, tightly corseted armchair, designed in 1958 for Plycraft, is a timeless design and sits well in any interior. It is still made today.

Wendell Castle has always designed iconic chairs. He prefers to call himself a "furniture artist." This is a sculpted oak chair with a hard leather sling seat. It was designed in 1963. 34.5in (87.5cm) high ★ ★ ★ ★ ★

once said: "To me the organic form offers the most exciting possibilities. It can never be completely understood in one glance." He began working in oak and walnut but was soon to move into plastics, in the 1960s.

Eero Saarinen designed many of the most recognizable pieces of furniture manufactured by the New York-based Knoll Furniture Company. These include his sculptural, organic Tulip chairs and tables, Womb and Grasshopper chairs, and the 70 series seating collection. Saarinen had studied with **Florence Knoll** (born Schust) and Charles and Ray Eames at the Cranbrook Academy of Art in Bloomfield Hills, Michigan, where his father was the director. The students there were encouraged to experiment, and in 1940 Saarinen and Charles Eames submitted revolutionary molded-plywood furniture designs to the Organic Design in Home Furnishing competition run by the Museum of Modern Art in New York. Their win ensured their influence on modern furniture design.

Charles and Ray Eames used molded plywood and plastic, wire mesh and fiberglass for their furniture. Perhaps their most celebrated design, the 670 lounge chair—a reinterpretation of the English club chair—and its accompanying 671 ottoman consists of a laminated-wood shell with deep leather upholstery.

Florence Schust and her husband, Hans Knoll, developed his furniture company into an international success, commissioning friends including Eero Saarinen, **Harry Bertoia**, and **Ludwig Mies van der Rohe**. Florence Knoll also designed elegant and well-proportioned furniture and introduced comprehensive design to office planning.

Another young designer, **George Nelson**, became the director of one of America's other large furniture companies: Herman Miller. Nelson had met many European designers while studying in Rome, and he was offered a job at Herman Miller when its president, D.J. DePree, saw his Storagewall modular shelving system in *Life* magazine.

As companies such as Knoll and Herman Miller grew, they started to take fewer creative risks. Consequently designers such as **Edward Wormley** looked to smaller businesses to commission their designs (in his case, the Indiana-based Dunbar Furniture Corporation). **Vladimir Kagan**, on the other hand, began working in his father's workshop. His father's mantra of "measure three times and cut once" was ignored by his son, who maintained that he cut three times and never measured. While Modernist design became the height of fashion in the United States in the post-war period, some designers pursued a design aesthetic closer to the Craftsman ideal. **George Nakashima** had trained as an architect, but after his internment during World War II he settled in New Hope, Pennsylvania, and began working with wood. His furniture depends on the inherent qualities of the material. He explored the organic expressiveness of wood and chose boards with knots, burls, and figured grain.

Sergio Rodrigues

Architect **Sergio Rodrigues** is considered to be one of the most important influences on modern design in Brazil. His company Oca Industry, which he started in Ipanema, Rio de Janeiro, in 1956, encouraged craft and furniture design in the country. But he left it after 12 years to focus on designing his own furniture.

Rodrigues used local woods such as eucalyptus, jacaranda, peroba, and imbuia, combined with leather and rattan in his furniture. His designs mixed Classical details with traditional woodworking skills and contemporary shapes and scale. Their unique character was created by a combination of natural and sensual characteristics. He came to international prominence when he launched the Poltrona Molé (soft armchair or Sheriff chair). The low-slung, wood-framed chair has leather cushions supported by straps that flow over the arms. It had been designed four years earlier, but in 1961 it won first prize at an international furniture competition in Cantu, Italy, where it was celebrated for being distinctively Brazilian in attitude, scale, and material. Early Molé chairs were made from jacaranda, but since the trees were over-harvested, the factory switched to using eucalyptus, pau marfim, and ivorywood.

In all, Rodrigues designed more than 1,200 pieces of furniture. Other notable pieces include the Taja line, a collection of outdoor chairs and tables, and the Voltaire armchair. The Voltaire has a solid wood frame, but its voluptuous upholstered seat and backrest seem to envelop the sitter. The Chifruda or "horned" chair has a sweeping wooden backrest that resembles a pair of antlers.

Sergio Rodrigues manages to combine the solidity of the jacaranda wood with the fineness of the design. A Brazilian high-backed jacaranda Cantu chair, with brown leather seat, one of a set of eight. c.1959 39.5in (100.5cm) high NPA

The 1960s rosewood bookshelf is almost a piece of sculpture – practical but beautiful. 63in (160cm) high NPA

The strong lines and deep color of this Sheriff coffee table, designed by **Sergio Rodrigues**, come from his use of native Brazilian tropical hardwood. 47.5in (120.5cm) wide ★ ★ ★ ★ ★

The **Sergio Rodrigues** bookshelves and chairs complement the industrial French 1930s dining table (*opposite*). The contemporary light ensures the retro look does not become too self-conscious.

Knoll

The company was founded by Hans Knoll in New York in 1916. He believed that architects would need good-quality streamlined furniture that would suit their Modernist buildings. He married Florence Schurst in 1946 and they formed Knoll Associates. Florence had degrees in architecture and design, but most importantly she had worked with and studied under **Eero Saarinen**, **Ludwig Mies van der Rohe**, **Marcel Breuer**, and **Walter Gropius**. She and Hans understood the importance of employing the best designers—the names—and they revolutionized mid-20th-century design by paying the designers a royalty and crediting their work. Not only did that ensure they would attract the best designers, but it also gave Knoll added prestige. In 1947, realizing they could not find the fabrics they wanted for their designs, they opened a textile showroom, which was an immediate success. Florence's assertion that "Good design is good business" has assured Knoll's success into the 21st century.

The enduring appeal of the furniture designed by Florence Knoll is its high quality and Modernist appeal. It fits in extremely well with open-plan interiors, which have clean, crisp, rectilinear lines. Florence was the creative hub of Knoll, insisting on the highest quality of design and instigating new production techniques. She also understood the benefit of buying the rights for Knoll to produce the iconic designs such luminaries as the pieces shown opposite designed by Mies van der Rohe and Breuer. Like so many of her groundbreaking designs that became the gold standard for the industry, the 1961 executive collection, including the series of credenzas, made its way into the pantheon of modern classics. Florence Knoll's designs are reserved and cool, severe and angular, reflecting the objective perfectionism of the period. As a pioneer of the Knoll Planning Unit, she revolutionized interior space-planning with her belief in "total design"—embracing all aspects of design principles that were radical departures from the standard practice in the 1950s, but which were quickly adopted and remain widely used today.

This staircase was designed with an iron frame and brackets and massive slabs of unfinished walnut. The wooden stool was designed by **Charlotte Perriand** and the chair was manufactured by Knoll in the 1940s.

Mies van der Rohe's daybed manages to applaud the Modernist principles with the walnut and polished-steel frame, while the leather cushion and bolster ensure comfort. 1929 79in (197.5cm) long ★ ★ ★ ★ ★ ★

A late 1940s/early '50s credenza designed by **Florence Knoll** imparts a strong modern feel while retaining something of a softer look with the seagrass-lined sliding doors. 72in (183cm) wide ★ ★ ★ ★ ★ ★

The Long chair, with its frame of laminated birch supporting the timber seat, was developed by **Marcel Breuer** in 1935. This one is from the 1950s. 51.25in (130cm) long ★ ★ ★ ★ ★ ★

The classic **Isamu Noguchi** teak rocking stool with innovative steel wire frame. Designed in 1954. 14in (35.5cm) wide ★ ★ ★ ★ ★ ★

Knoll developed the trend for wire furniture, encouraging designers such as **Warren Platner**. This set, 1725, was designed in 1966. 27.5in (70cm) high ★ ★ ★ ★ ★ ★

Florence Knoll's 10-drawer credenza combines the depth of color of the rosewood with a finely grained marble top. 1963 74.5in (189cm) long ★ ★ ★ ★ ★ ★

The Scandinavian aesthetic

The roots of the Scandinavian aesthetic can be traced back to the 1930s. **Kaare Klint** was a Danish architect and furniture designer, known as the father of modern Danish furniture design. His style was epitomized by clean, pure lines, the use of top-quality materials and superb craftsmanship. As a result of the furniture school he founded at the Royal Academy in 1924, Klint had a strong influence on Danish furniture, shaping the work of designers such as **Poul Kjærholm** and **Børge Mogensen**. Notable examples of his work include the Safari chair and the Deck chair (both 1933).

In the 1950s the work of Scandinavian designers garnered increasing praise as their designs reached an international audience. Buyers were inspired by their minimal version of the Modern look that paradoxically relied on traditional techniques and materials, especially teak for furniture.

During that decade the Danish architect and furniture designer **Finn Juhl** won five gold medals for his work at Milan Triennale shows. The publicity this brought extended to other Scandinavian designers. Juhl had hoped to be an art historian, and his admiration for tradition is evident in the sculptural forms he created with cabinetmaker **Niels Vodder**. Pieces such as his Chieftains chair reveal inspirations as far-reaching as abstract art and organic, natural forms.

In the 1940s, fellow Dane Børge Mogensen was head of the Danish Cooperative Wholesale Society. This gave him a comprehensive knowledge of manufacturing and retail. His later work was influenced both by this and by his early fascination with the work of Kaare Klint, an architect and designer who was interested in both Classical design and ergonomics. The result was elegant

In the Scandinavian aesthetic, exposed wooden frames, as in this set of upholstered Danish furniture in a mid-1950s sitting room, almost invariably play as much of an aesthetic role as a structural one.

A Safari chair, designed by the "father of Scandinavian design," **Kaare Klint**, has a canvas back and seat with leather strap arms, stained beech frame. A variation of the campaign chair, it was designed in 1933. 31.5in (80cm) high ★ ★ ★ ★ ★

Functional is the word that best describes **Børge Mogensen**'s design. The majority of his furniture was designed with industrial production in mind, and is characterized by strong and simple lines. This sideboard is made from palisander wood. c.1958 93.7in (238cm) long ★ ★ ★ ★ ★

modern-yet-traditional furniture, mostly made from wood, which reached a wide audience. Typical pieces include the 1954 Boligens Byggeskabe cabinet system, which had smooth, clean lines with discreet hinges and handles.

Another celebrated Danish designer, **Hans Wegner**, saw his work as the "continuous process of purification." His celebrated Wishbone chair, with its characteristic Y-shaped back, could be dismissed as just another light, comfortable dining chair, but it is recognized as a triumph of craftsmanship. It takes more than 100 steps to make, and the hand-woven seat requires more than 131 yards (120m) of paper cord. It was designed for Carl Hansen & Søn in 1949, went into production in 1950, and is still being made today.

In typically Scandinavian fashion, most of Poul Kjærholm's Danish contemporaries opted for wood as their primary furniture construction material. Kjærholm engineered a shift in the Scandinavian modern tradition by combining traditionally exceptional Danish woodworking with emerging technologies for employing steel and aluminum in designing his sophisticated, elegant, and architectural furniture. His subtle use of stainless-steel rods and polished-steel frames enhanced the natural elements rather than overpowered them. In doing so he created nearly a dozen iconic pieces of 20th-century design.

In his work Kjærholm always combined steel with other, softer materials such as wood, leather, cane, or marble. He stated that "Steel's constructive potential is not the only thing that interests me; the refraction of light on its surface is an important part of my artistic work. I consider steel a material with the same artistic merit as wood and leather."

Poul Henningsen based his design on analysis of lampshade function: the size, shape and position of the shades determine light and glare. His Louvre, Kugle, and Artichoke lamps are available in re-edition from Louis Poulsen. Originals like this one are highly collectible.

One of the most iconic chairs ever designed is the Ant Chair, designed by **Arne Jacobsen** in 1952 for Fritz Hansen. He said: "I found that people needed a new type of chair for the small kitchen dinettes that are found in most new buildings today, a little, light, and inexpensive chair." 30in (76cm) high
★ ★ ★ ★ ★

Danish ceramist **Axel Salto** is known for stoneware characterized by earthen colors and botanical forms. This vase was designed by Salto in 1957. He had won the Grand Prix at the Milan Triennale in 1951. 3.5in (9cm) high ★ ★ ★ ★ ★

The work of **Arne Jacobsen** is characterized by its fluidity, precision, and logical construction. For example, his iconic Ant chair, designed in 1952, consists of a molded plywood seat supported by three tubular stainless-steel legs. This made it easy to mass produce—fulfilling its brief as a seat for a factory canteen. The Series 7 chairs followed the style. Over six million of the basic Series 7 chair (the 3107 is similar to the Ant, except that it has four legs rather than three) have been made, making it possibly the most popular chair ever designed.

The Finnish designer **Yrjö Kukkapuro** designed the famous Karuselli chair in 1963. The chair owes its name to the Finnish word for carousel, which describes the way it swivels and rocks. Kukkapuro had been experimenting with fiberglass for some time, thinking it the ideal material for a chair. He said: "A chair should be as softly shaped as people are and if at all possible, just as beautiful."

The combination of modern and traditional extended to Scandinavian ceramics. Some firms publicized their wares—and encouraged their designers—by opening galleries where the public could view the latest designs. The Finnish company Arabia opened a studio in 1932 to allow its designers to work away from the pressures of the factory environment. It proved to be a successful venture, and the Swedish pottery Gustavsberg followed its example in 1942.

Gustavsberg's studio produced wares that were influenced by the spirit of the Bauhaus and was key to the golden age of Swedish ceramic design that lasted into the 1950s. **Stig Lindberg** was the leading light at the studio, and he became the company's artistic director in 1947, a role he held until 1957, and again from 1972 until 1978. At the studio he was able to explore the decorative and sculptural properties of both clay and glazes. The first range he developed there was fresh and new but also reflected its Scandinavian roots. He used bright colors (including multi-colored teardrops), modern designs, and curving forms such as dishes and vases shaped like curving leaves or buds. His work in the 1950s features a more subdued, monochrome palette such as the Domino range, which comprised simple, clean-lined shapes covered with a myriad of rows of white triangles on a black background.

This brown leather Karuselli chair was designed by **Yrjö Kukkapuro** of Finland. Its shape was based on the shape of his body when he had fallen in the snow. c.1965 36in (91.5cm) high ★ ★ ★ ★ ★ new and with matching ottoman

Swedish glass

The Scandinavian aesthetic had a global impact. Scandinavian glass from this time features flawless surfaces, cool colors, and organic shapes. **Ingeborg Lundin** was the first female designer to work for Orrefors in Sweden. Her Apple vase, designed c.1957, has become an icon of mid-20th-century Scandinavian glass: its modest beauty and functional simplicity led to it being described as the "Swedish Grace." The body has thinly blown walls and a neck that resembles an apple stalk. Like other designers from the region, she combined color and form to make subtle suggestions of the Scandinavian landscape.

Lundin's designs were simple, but they could be made only by the most skilled craftsmen, as they pushed the possibilities of fragile glass to the limit. The Apple vase was created for the influential Helsingborg 55 exhibition, and remains a symbol of the golden age of Swedish art glass. It earned Lundin the title "the Balenciaga of glass."

Vicke Lindstrand was possibly the leading figure in mid-century Scandinavian glass. He is renowned for his plain, natural, curving shapes using clear, colorless glass with heavily stylized engraving and cut design. His glass for Kosta Boda in the early 1950s featured textured ribbing, spiraling stripes, and engraved designs that exploit his skill as an illustrator.

Timo Sarpaneva joined the Finnish firm Iittala in 1950 and played a crucial role in transforming glass from a domestic necessity to a sculptural art form. His work used bubbles and textured surfaces, sometimes contrasting with clear, unblemished areas. His textured Finlandia range, first made in 1963, calls to mind two distinctive features of the Scandinavian landscape—tree bark and cracked ice.

The Finnish glassworks Nuutajärvi Nöstjö benefitted from the austere geometric designs of **Kaj Franck**, one of the leading figures of Finnish design between 1940 and 1980. He has been described as the "conscience of Finnish design," for his removal of all extraneous ornament from his designs. Many of the pieces of glass he designed contained elongated trapped air bubbles. Franck's art glass was inspired by the Finnish winters and was challenging to make.

A 1950–60s Gustavsburg Leaf faience dish, with applied branch and leaf handle, designed by **Stig Lindberg** in 1940. The natural form is typical of his work. 4.75in (12cm) long ★ ★ ★ ★ ★ ★

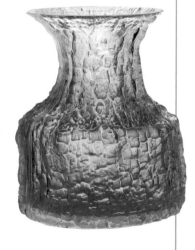

An Orrefors Apple vase, designed by **Ingeborg Lundin** in 1955. Launched at the Milan Triennale it was lauded as a landmark design. 15in (37cm) high ★ ★ ★ ★ ★ ★

A Kosta tapering ovoid vase, designed by **Vicke Lindstrand** in 1955, with internal spirals of burgundy. 6.25in (16cm) high ★ ★ ★ ★ ★ ★

An Iittala Finlandia mold blown vase with a varied textured finish, designed by **Timo Sarpaneva** in 1964. This range was originally made using molds lined with real bark. 7in (17cm) high ★ ★ ★ ★ ★ ★

A **Kaj Franck** vase, for Nuutajärvi Nöstjö, with rows of elongated bubbles, dated 1953. 3.25in (8cm) high ★ ★ ★ ★ ★ ★

Poul Kjærholm

Poul Kjærholm (1929–80) began as a cabinetmaker's apprentice with Gronbech in 1948, before going on to the Danish School of Arts and Crafts in Copenhagen in 1952, where he was tutored by **Hans Wegner**. He subsequently went on to teach there until 1956. His further academic career led him from being appointed lecturer at the Royal Danish Academy of Fine Arts in 1959 to head of the Institute of Design in 1973 and finally to professorship in 1976.

Kjærholm's signature design combination of steel and aluminum with traditional materials such as wood and leather produced dozens of chairs, long chairs, stools, and tables that became landmarks for Danish furniture design, including the famous PK22 chair and the PK24 long chair. His work has often been described as "modest in means, but rich in expression." Kjærholm's design is characterized by its understated elegance, clean lines and remarkable attention to detail. Although he always considered functionality an absolute requirement, this was always combined with a reluctance to compromise his vision as an artist. He was a true master of making a problematic production process appear effortless in the finished piece of furniture.

From the mid-1950s Kjærholm worked for Ejvind Kold Christensen, an entrepreneur who gave him tremendous artistic freedom and who produced an extensive range of his furniture. Kjærholm's distinctive style is evident as early as 1952 in his PKO minimalist plywood series of furniture. The PK61 coffee table of 1955 has an illogical supporting frame that is visible through the glass top.

In 1958 Kjærholm attracted international acclaim for his contribution to the Formes Scandinaves exhibition held in Paris and his receipt of the legendary Lunning Prize for Scandinavian designers in the same year for his PK22 chair. In both 1957 and 1960 he won the Grand Prize at the Milan Triennale. His work is best encapsulated in the words of his contemporary **Gerrit Rietveld**: "Poul Kjærholm is a man whose modern, functionalistic approaches keep all extravagant tendencies towards luxury at bay."

A vintage daybed by Poul Kjærholm sits in front of a monumental black granite fireplace in this modern living room.

A PK24 chaise longue, hammock model, with polished steel frame, woven cane and black leather headrest. Designed in 1965, it is manufactured by Fritz Hansen. It is the perfect marriage of industrial style and soft modernism. 61in (155cm) long ★★★★★★

The PK33 stool is chromium-plated steel and plywood with a leather cushion. 1959 14in (35.5cm) high ★★★★★★

A PK27 easy chair designed in 1970 for E. Kold Christensen. It has an ash frame and leather seat pad. 39.5in (100cm) wide ★★★★★★

A rare and early Molded Aluminum chair, manufactured by Chris Sørensen. 1953 25in (63cm) high ★★★★★★

Poul Kjærholm's classic "Scandinavian modern" dining chairs retain their timeless elegance at a contemporary zinc table.

The modernity of Mid-Century designs means that they work well in modern interiors. These 1950s chairs by **Poul Kjærholm** and the table by **Mies van der Rohe** sit happily with modern art (*above*).

Scandinavian designers favored natural materials and the sculptured, elegant furniture they produced had a more human feel than the cold, metallic quality of pre-war Modern design. **Poul Kjærholm** embraced both ideologies. In the main living room in his home in Denmark, designed by his wife, Hanne, he effortlessly embraced furniture in wood, leather, steel, and laminate. The look is further softened by the natural sisal flooring, white painted walls, and natural beams (*left*).

Finn Juhl

Pelikan chair 1940
Chieftains chair 1949

The Danish architect and industrial and interior designer **Finn Juhl** was born in 1912 and died in 1989. Having studied architecture at the Royal Danish Academy of Fine Arts from 1930 to 1934, he spent 10 years working at Vilhelm Lauritzen's architectural firm before establishing his own design practice in Nyhavn, Copenhagen, in 1945. Stand-out state and commercial projects from the designer credited with introducing the "Danish Modern" style to America are the interior of the Danish national broadcaster's Radio Building, the Trusteeship Council Chamber at the United Nations in New York (1951–52), and numerous designs for the ceramics manufacturer Bing & Grøndahl, the silversmith **Georg Jensen**, and Scandinavian Airlines—including aircraft interiors for the last of these. However, the ergonomic and aesthetic principles that underpinned Juhl's work are best represented in his furniture designs, and in two chairs in particular.

The first of these—the Pelikan—was designed in 1940, and so named because it resembled in profile the outstretched-wing form of a pelican, bird native to Finland. Although its avant-garde design was met with hostility in some quarters—one conservative critic described it as looking more like a "tired walrus"—it gained international acclaim. Strongly influenced by contemporary abstract art, especially the work of the German sculptor Jean (Hans) Arp, it proved to be at the cutting edge of the organic, sculptural forms that came to dominate mid-20th-century furniture design. Moreover, the seemingly one-piece upholstered reclining seat and curvaceous, embracing back, raised on four sturdy, raked wooden legs, were welcoming and comfortable—qualities ensured not only by the ergonomics of the design, but also by the high standard of construction (initially by cabinetmaker Niels Vodder; nowadays by Hansen & Sorensen).

Above all, the Pelikan represented a move away from the out-and-out functionalism of early Modernist designs, and reinstated form as something in its own right—in this case sculptural and birdlike organic—rather than a mere follower of function. In 1948 Juhl reinforced this design rationale with his Chieftains chair. Also highly sculptural, also supremely comfortable, the shapes of its precision-crafted hardwood frame, and its padded leather seat, back,

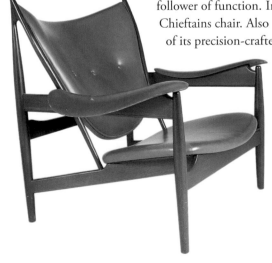

and armrests individually recall the weaponry (shields and spears) and collectively recall the thrones of tribal societies. Indeed, aside from his insightful observation that "one cannot create happiness with beautiful objects, but one can spoil quite a lot of happiness with bad ones," it is perhaps this elevation of symbolism over function as a generator of form that is Juhl's greatest contribution to mid-20th-century design and beyond.

The Chieftains is regarded as the catalyst for the breakthrough of Danish Modern in the U.S. in the 1950s. 38in (95cm) high ★★ ☆ ☆ ☆

Finn Juhl's Pelikan is manufactured by Hansen & Sorensen, but the first four were made by Niels Vodder and are highly desirable. Three are accounted for, but one has yet to be found!

Influential pieces

Materials such as ply- and laminated woods, which could be molded into flowing shapes, encouraged designers to search for the perfect form. The result was a number of pieces of furniture that at the time were considered to be experimental and even revolutionary. But their clean lines and organic contours have resulted in their becoming celebrated as modern classics with a far-reaching influence. Some chairs combine these new shapes with sleek upholstery for increased comfort without compromising their modern edge. Others rely on their sculptural form for their appeal. Many of these designs were created with mass production in mind, and as a result many examples have been made. They have also been copied and used as the inspiration for other forms.

The **Eero Saarinen** birch plywood Grasshopper chair was designed for Knoll in 1946. Visually light, yet incredibly sturdy, the Grasshopper, with its lean and angular lines, seems to float effortlessly. It was reintroduced by Modernica in 1995. 34in (86cm) high ★★ ★ ★ ★ ★ new

The visually exciting **George Nelson** Pretzel chair was designed in 1957. It was produced by Herman Miller in plywood and vinyl. This rare chair was produced for just one year. 30.5in (77.5cm) high NPA

A simple classic. The molded-ply LCW (Lounge Chair Wood) chair, designed by **Charles** and **Ray Eames**. This design earned them recognition from *Time* magazine as The Best Design of the 20th Century. *Time* called the design "something elegant, light and comfortable. Much copied but never bettered." 1945 29in (77.4cm) ★★ ★ ★ ★ ★ new

An American lounge chair and ottoman, designed by **Charles** and **Ray Eames** in 1956, models 670 and 671. Charles said he wanted this chair to have the "warm receptive look of a well-used baseman's mitt." Chair 32in (81cm) high ★★ ★ ★ ★ ★ new

This elegant wall-hung cabinet by **George Nakashima** forms an essential part of the composition of the art on the wall. Its vertical slats, horizontal form, and rich wooden tones attractively balance the whole room. Freeing up floor space adds to the overall framing.

A **Finn Juhl** teak and cane credenza perfectly encapsulates the warmth and human scale of the Scandinavian aesthetic (*above*). It was designed in 1950 for Baker. 78in (198cm) wide ★★ ★ ★ ★ ★

The simple juxtaposition of the walnut drawers makes this dresser, designed by **Gio Ponti** for Singer & Sons, a Mid-Century Modern classic (*right*). c.1950 47in (119cm) wide ★★★ ★ ★ ★

This rare Edward Wormley Oregon pine dresser with drawers over sliding doors shows that the influence of soft modernism was not exclusively Scandinavian (*below*). It was designed in the 1950s for Dunbar. 34in (86.5cm) high ★★ ★ ★ ★ ★

An ISA Sheriff sofa, designed by **Sergio Rodrigues** in tropical hardwood with black leather cushions (*above*). Designed in 1957, it is the perfect example of comfort and style. 81in (205cm) wide ★★ ★ ★ ★ ★

The Wishbone Chair is perhaps **Hans Wegner**'s most celebrated work (*left*). Despite its straightforward appearance, it takes more than 100 steps to make one. Wegner designed the chair for Carl Hansen in 1949, and it has been in continuous production since 1950. 29.5in (75cm) high ★ ★ ★ ★ ★ ★

The classic light of the 1960s, **Poul Henningsen**'s copper and chrome-plated steel Artichoke ceiling lamp employs leaflike elements to compose the form (*top right*). With its grand size, the Artichoke creates atmospheric lighting for larger domestic spaces.1965 Body 30in (76cm) diameter ★★ ★ ★ ★ ★

When a craftsman designs a piece of furniture that is stylish, comfortable and hence desirable, it is destined to be a timeless classic. This **Hans Wegner** oak, teak and cane chaise lounge is such a piece (*above right*). c.1950 60in (152.5cm) long ★ ★ ★ ★ ★ ★

The glorious lines of this 1950s **Vladimir Kagan** floating seat and back sofa are dictated by the sculptural walnut legs (*right*). 80in (203cm) wide ★ ★★ ★ ★ ★

Naturally comfortable

Interiors filled with natural, organic furnishings offered homeowners a break with the past. Gone were the heavy furniture and cluttered shelves of their parents' and grandparents' generation, to be replaced by a pared-back room filled with light and that allowed the furniture and accessories to speak for themselves. Simplicity is the key to this style of interior, and the result is modern sophistication. A few choice pieces of furniture—rather than a crowded collection—add to the effect.

The most effective backdrops are fuss-free. Plain, painted walls make an ideal setting for classic pieces of furniture, or use polished wood panels or period wallpaper to add color and interest. Cool colors such as blues and grays are perfect, highlighted with pinks, greens, and yellows. Decorate the walls with a few well-chosen paintings or a piece of wall sculpture, rather than lots of artwork.

Allow light to permeate the room—and enhance the elegant proportions of the furniture—by keeping window treatments to a minimum. Use simple drapes in plain or period fabrics, or vertical or horizontal shades.

Fabrics in the form of rugs and upholstery add color and texture to otherwise plain surfaces. Create further visual interest by including pieces of ceramics and glass or wooden sculpture, displayed on simple, modular shelving.

Lighting is key to the success of these interiors. Plain pendant shades hang from the ceiling, enhanced by sculptural floor and table lamps. The overall effect should one of be comfort, with light and clean lines.

Fifties style can express both modernity and individuality. In architect Michael Wolfson's dining room the set of T chairs were designed by **William Katavolos**, **Ross Littell**, and **Douglas Kelley** in 1952. With their chromed-steel and enameled-steel frames and leather swing seats, they perfectly display the Modern movement's geometric formalism, but with a softened edge.

So much of retro style is about experimenting with texture (*above*). In this living room the textured wood paneling contrasts with the shag pile carpet. A perfect setting for the 1970s chairs and table.

This rare original leather High Wingback from the 1940s by the Danish designer **Frits Henningsen** creates a sense of style in any room (*right*). With clear inspiration from earlier epochs, such as French imperial style and 18th-century British furniture, Frits Henningsen created a timeless classic by merging the traditional with the contemporary.

In a very modern Florida house, with a sliding glass door leading to the outdoor swimming pool, the vintage elements feel right at home (*opposite*). With the **George Nelson** Bubble lamp and the **Alvar Aalto**-style cantilevered rocker, the interior is comfortable and stylish.

In a small dining area a print by Candida Hofer hangs on a wall next to a **Jean Prouvé** table and **Charles** and **Ray Eames** dining chairs (*left*).

Resting on a Japanese slate floor in a light-filled room, this large central-pedestal dining table was designed by **Eero Saarinen** and the chairs by **Eames**. All are classics of shape and style (*below*).

In this dining room an **Eero Saarinen** marble-topped Tulip table is surrounded by **Arne Jacobsen** 3107 chairs, in a variety of materials and colors (*opposite*).

Classics go well with classics. Many people have different styles of late 18th-century dining chairs round the table, so why not try the same design trick with Mid-Century chairs? The **Eero Saarinen** tulip table holds it all together (*above*).

Contrasted with white walls and a black hearth, accented with tones of blue, yellow, and green in the soft furnishings and artwork, and complemented by bare wooden floorboards, a Mid-Century Ercol side-table and upholstered armchair and stool fashioned in teak bring the organic, warm brown tones of the forest into this light and airy sitting room (*opposite*).

The eclectic mix of styles makes a dramatic statement in art director Jean-Christophe Aumas's Paris apartment. The room is full of visual delight with the colors, seating, industrial lighting and funky objects. The Scandinavian chaise in the middle is modern but has a decidedly Mid-Century feel. Against the wall is an original vintage Swan sofa designed by **Arne Jacobsen** in 1958 and produced by Fritz Hansen. The charismatic three-dimensional shape contains no straight lines but is rather based on curves.

There is a pleasing juxtaposition of old and new in this apartment (*right*). The distressed, grand, painted 18th-century paneling and stripped floorboards provide a perfect backdrop for the 1950s **Arne Jacobsen** chair. The original leather of the chair is also showing pleasing signs of age.

In this open-plan living space there are various zoned areas for sitting, sleeping, cooking, and eating (*below*). The funky 1970s industrial chairs in the foreground set the scene.

Berlin meets Brazil

In a fashionable area in East Berlin there is a little enclave of exotic Rio de Janeiro. The interior designer Hubert Zandberg has a passion for the furniture and traditions of Mid-Century Brazil. Historically many Brazilian designers had been trained in Europe and were influenced by the "old country" styles. This began to change in the early 20th century and by the mid-20th century the work of **Joaquim Tenreiro**, **Sergio Rodrigues**, and **José Zanine Caldas** had transformed Brazilian design. In this apartment the Brazilian pieces, with indigenous woods, combine effortlessly with Scandinavian brass lights, tubular steel Bauhaus chairs, a **Jean Prouvé** industrial bench, and contemporary Italian tables. The designer believes that there should be a mix of styles, as to have all retro or vintage can become too self-conscious. There are also large photographs of the semi-desert South African Karoo by David Goldblatt that take Zandberg back to his rural South African roots. It is in the contrast that you achieve the dynamic.

A cocktail trolley was an absolutely essential accessory in any stylish Mid-Century apartment. This, however, is a rather fine example designed by the Brazilian **Sergio Rodrigues** (*below*). The mood is lightened by the kitsch paraphernalia, including a pineapple ice bucket.

The perfect mix of natural and industrial (*right*)—the Brazilian jacaranda-wood chair with rare color combination Kuba fabric to the iconic **Jean Prouvé** steel and oak bench.

Cubism dominates this room (*opposite*). The structure of blocks is at the heart of Modernism. The sofa is Brazilian with African fabric that is Modernist-inspired, the brass table bought in Istanbul is Italian, and the brass brandy glass-shaped light is Scandinavian.

In the library again (*above*) is a pleasing mix of styles, from the French Business Class metal and cane chair to the small plywood Spanish 1950s kidney-shaped table to the fascinating collections of African artifacts on the shelves, showing the influence of primitivism.

This chair is designed by the Brazilian **Joaquim Tenreiro**, a pioneer of modernist Brazilian furniture-making (*left*). He said a chair should be "formally light ... a lightness which has nothing to do with weight itself, but with graciousness, and the functionality of spaces."

In the mid-1950s **Charles** and **Ray Eames's** Lounge Chair (670) and Ottoman (671) revived the classic combination of armchair and matching footstool. This contemporary black leather-upholstered example combines an Eames-like ottoman with a Mid-Century Modern interpretation of the traditional "wing-back" design (*below*).

In the corner of the bedroom an open armchair designed by **Rodrigues** is in front of a 1950s French desk (*opposite*). Zandberg says the ball light is very "Berlin" and also like the moon in Africa. The photograph is by David Goldblatt of rural Africa, where Zandberg grew up.

Utility

The exposed wood, brickwork, and concrete found in converted warehouses and factories call for bold furnishings that match the drama of these unique living spaces. Tables and shelving made from reclaimed wood—or oversized pieces from factories or grand country houses, which are too large for modern homes—provide a contrast to sleek designer chairs and dramatic, modern lighting, which become the centerpieces of these high-ceilinged rooms. The stripped-back effect lets the materials speak for themselves and allows wooden beams and doors, concrete floors, and stone columns—the skeleton of the building, in other words—to stand back and create light, airy rooms. Enhance all this with pieces of dramatic wall art, colorful rugs, and simple fireplaces. The result is ideal for uncluttered, open-plan living, especially when teamed with an industrial-style stainless-steel kitchen and simple, light drapes.

Located in Paris's 10th arrondissement, near to the Porte Saint-Denis, this loft space dates from the 1880s. Exposed brick and rough cement form the perfect background for a distressed 19th-century French glazed cabinet and a metal table with later 20th-century school chairs.

In this converted 1830s church, simple muslin drapes do not detract from the huge scale of the impressive windows. The massive refectory table is similarly attended by white Ant chairs (*below*).

Architects Olivier Martin and Virginie Gravière say their remit in this old hay storeroom was to "domesticate the space without removing its brute force" (*opposite*). They have done that by keeping many of the original features and choosing simple utilitarian furniture that does not detract from the overall effect.

Retro mix

Combining retro pieces from different eras creates characterful interiors filled with color and interest. These happy mixes of styles often work best when they eschew designer names in favor of objects that simply look good together. The result may not always be cohesive, but it will be lively and imaginative.

There is no need to concentrate on pieces in one style, in fact the more elements that are included in each room the better. To help to bring the theme of a room together, use high-contrast colors. One or more combined with white will add additional bursts of color and create a backdrop for any eclectic collection.

Combine functional, decorative furniture with reclaimed advertising signs and accessories. Retro-styled technology such as radios, food processors, and refrigerators adds to the effect. The result is unique collections that are never neutral, and always fascinating.

This type of chair, with its chrome frame and brightly lacquered seat and back, is an example of mass-produced Modernist design found not only in homes but also in coffee bars and cafés in the late 1950s and early 1960s (*above*). It was a period when architects and designers believed that good design should be available to all.

The styles of the 1950s and '60s are finding a ready audience again. The austerity furniture of the post war era has been revalued. These 1950s English Rose kitchen cabinets with melamine tops create a good retro look and are still inexpensive (*left*).

Color is important in creating any style. After the war, homeowners longed for color in their lives, and designers provided it. This interior has a good rustic mix overseen by the 1950s poster. The 19th-century French bergère is given new life by the cheerful lighthouse-print fabric, and the rustic chairs by bright pillows (*opposite*).

The Diamond chair designed by **Harry Bertoia** in 1952 is still as popular today as it was then. Here it reflects the warm color of the chimney and the natural Berber carpet on which it sits.

Wire furniture

The commercial success of furniture made from plastic, molded plywood, and other sculptural materials encouraged designers to revisit metal tubes as a material for making modern, elegant furniture. The results were new and exciting, and a departure from the chrome-plated designs of the Bauhaus and other Art Deco movements. **Charles** and **Ray Eames** and **Poul Kjærholm** were among the designers who used metal frames and supports as part of their designs, but **Harry Bertoia** and **Warren Platner** took things further.

Bertoia's wire furniture collection, designed for Knoll Associates in the early 1950s, was a phenomenal success—so successful that the Italian-born American was able to give up furniture design to concentrate on sculpture for the rest of his life. The Diamond chair (model 421LU) is probably the best-known piece: a molded square of vinyl-coated steel-rod mesh is set on a steel-rod frame, while a pad cushion provides comfort. The revolutionary construction meant that, as Bertoia explained, the chairs were "made mainly of air." Many of Bertoia's sculptures also used metal rods, arranged in rows, some capped with cylinders or discs, that play a kind of music when touched by the hand or blown in the wind.

The American architect and designer Warren Platner went one step further. His 1966 collection for Knoll included a set of tables and stools described in the catalogue as being like sheaves of wheat. Each piece consisted of hundreds of hand-welded nickel-plated stainless-steel rods. He described his inspiration thus: "I felt there was room for the kind of decorative gentle kind of design that appeared in a period style like Louis XV … but with a Rational base."

The American-Japanese sculptor and designer **Isamu Noguchi** used his eye for space and form to design refined and simple furniture for American manufacturers such as Knoll and Herman Miller. His c.1955 Cyclone table for Knoll features a circular laminate top on a base of intersecting V-shaped steel-wire supports. In the 1950s and '60s he also combined a metal base with traditional Japanese mino-gami paper made from the bark of mulberry trees to make a series of Akari light sculptures based on the ancient skills of Gifu lantern-makers. His sculptural lamps use electric light, while the traditional Japanese forms use candles.

Another successful metal chair was designed by the Dane **Verner Panton** for his parents' restaurant in the Komigen guesthouse in a small provincial town in Denmark. The Cone chair is a simple geometric form constructed from sheet metal and upholstered with foam and cotton. The chair, designed in 1958, is mounted on a stainless-steel swivel base so that it pivots. It went into production after a local entrepreneur spotted it, and it caused a sensation when it went on sale in New York—when the crowds staring at it in a shop window blocked the pavement, the police demanded that it be removed.

Before World War II, wire and metal furniture was the preserve of avant-garde interiors and the epitome of Modern design. But in the 1950s designers revisited it to create organic styles that almost seemed to float in thin air. They were ideal for the new style of interior that made the most of the natural light provided by floor-to-ceiling windows in many new homes. These new wire designs provided a contrast to the wooden floors and rooms decorated with deep-pile rugs, minimal shelving and storage systems, and stoneware popular at the time.

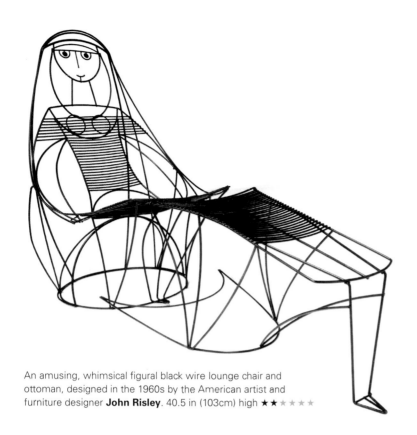

An amusing, whimsical figural black wire lounge chair and ottoman, designed in the 1960s by the American artist and furniture designer **John Risley**. 40.5 in (103cm) high ★★★★★

The classic DKR or Wire chair designed by **Charles** and **Ray Eames** has an "Eiffel Tower" base with splayed legs. It was designed in 1951 and in 1952 was awarded the Trail Blazer Award by the Home Fashions League of America. 31.75in (81cm) high ★★★★★★ replicas

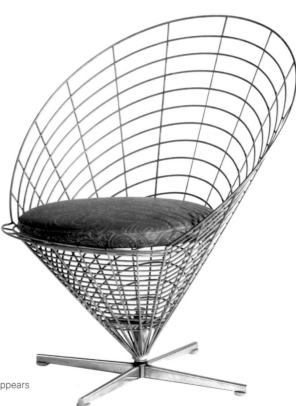

A pair of **Verner Panton** wire Cone chairs. The body of the chair is made of intertwined, spot-welded steel wire. The wire grid ensures that the armchair appears transparent, elegant and light. 1958 25in (63.5cm) wide ★★★★★ replicas

In the 1950s **Harry Bertoia** designed five wire pieces that became known as the Bertoia Collection for Knoll. Among these was the famous Diamond chair and bar stool shown here in different interiors, its fluid, sculptural forms made from a welded lattice of steel (*opposite and below*). In Bertoia's own words, "If you look at these chairs, they are mainly made of air, like sculpture. Space passes right through them." The Bertoia Collection is recognized worldwide as one of the great achievements of 20th-century furniture design.

The aesthetic and commercial success of Bertoia's Diamond range inspired many "lookalikes." This unattributed pair, with overtly conical seat frames, exploits the suitability of the steel wire mesh construction, with seat covers removed, for exterior use (*right*).

COLORFUL

In the 1950s and '60s new materials allowed designers to experiment with color. The new plastics and laminates held almost any shade and could be used to make exciting new shapes of furniture, or to add bursts of color to contrast with plain wooden surfaces. Brightly colored upholstery in the form of chair covers and pillows was also used to enhance fashionable modern interiors. Colored glass reflected the country where it was made: Scandinavian factories used clear glass and pale blues and greens inspired by icy landscapes, while Italian designers used the bright colors associated with Murano glass to create modern pieces using traditional techniques.

opposite, clockwise from top left The blocks of color on these open shelves are reminiscent of the wall unit ESU 420-C designed by **Charles** and **Ray Eames**. This immediately gives the room a vintage 1950s style. / The white Eames chair, with its "Eiffel Tower" base, contrasts with the candy-colored palette. / Glass from the 1960s and '70s—from **Ronald Stennett-Willson** at Kings Lynn to Murano and Bohemia— always looks better with natural light. / In a 19th-century country house, the dining room is transformed by a long pine table surrounded by colorful **Arne Jacobsen** Ant chairs.

right Once described by the art critic Dave Hickey as, among other attributes, "a California artist with Bauhaus tendencies," Jim Isermann makes paintings and wall-hangings that embrace the abstract but formal, often large-scale, post-World War II use of strong, vibrant color as both art and decoration.

Alessandro Pianon designed the whimsical Pulcino bird in 1961 for Vetreria Vistosi. The colorful orange-red and fused crushed glass with murine eyes and legs of hammered copper wire is typical of the sense of fun that characterized some post-war Murano designs. 8.5in (21.5cm) high ★ ★ ★ ★ ★ ★

A gray world made vibrant

The new forms and materials available after World War II war inspired many designers to bring color and new shapes into their work. The result was many original, era-defining pieces that look as modern—even futuristic—today as they did when they were first produced.

Glass manufacturers around the world were inspired to create new ranges that reflected the latest trends. In the United States, Blenko was among the most innovative. Designer **Winslow Anderson** worked with William H. Blenko Jr. to create a new range of vases and tablewares. Between 1948 and 1953 Anderson created a sculptural Horn vase and a decanter (known as the 948), which had a bent neck that was the result of a fortunate accident on the blowing floor. After 1953 **Wayne Husted** developed oversized, colorful pieces with large, sculptural stoppers.

Italian designers found different ways to challenge the possibilities of glass. On the island of Murano, designers such as **Dino Martens** and **Alessandro Pianon** reinvigorated traditional glassmaking techniques. For the Oriente range Martens designed in the 1940s for Aureliano Toso, he combined pinwheel murrines, bright enamel colors, and metal inclusions to produce glass with bright, abstract designs. Other pieces were whimsical. Pianon's stylized Pulcino birds for Vetreria Vistosi are charming and humorous ornaments, but also show immense glassmaking skill, from the textured surface to the applied murrine eyes and applied copper wire legs.

Despite the restrictions of working behind the Iron Curtain, Czech designers were free to experiment with modern versions of traditional designs or completely new styles. Some of these can be mistaken for Muranese designs from the same era, but many show a dynamism that is unique to Czech glass.

In the 1950s and '60s the Skrdlovice glassworks founded by **Emanuel Beránek** created heavy, thick-walled cased glass pieces with dynamic, curving lobed or spiraled surfaces which create optical effects. Similar techniques were used by **Josef Hospodka** at the Chribská glassworks. He created budlike organic forms. Curved organic forms, with applied colored blobs or trails of glass were made by **Frantisek Zemek**.

Many designers turned their backs on classic, 19th-century cut-glass designs to decorate glass with modern geometric cuts. Particularly notable are "lens" cut vases where the cut is both a motif and a window into the design, reflecting other cuts across the body.

On the other side of the Iron Curtain, potteries in West Germany finished ceramics with bold orange, red and green glazes contrasted with brown and beige. These were used to create molded stylized patterns, symbols, or surfaces that almost appear like rock or made from "bubbling" volcanic lava. Fashionable from the 1950s until the 1970s, these pieces by factories such as Scheurich and Roth retain the ability to turn heads.

The work of the Italian ceramicist **Marcello Fantoni** became known around the world from the 1950s to the 1970s. He used both bright and earth colors on matte, textured surfaces to create formal, sculptured pieces as well as those inspired by ancient Etruscan finds.

Designer Jonathan Adler's collection of 1960s Murano glass is humorous, colorful and unexpected against the white walls and fireplaces in a traditional room (*opposite*).

Bright colors and extraordinary shapes were also hallmarks of the work of the German industrial designer **Luigi Colani**. His plastic furniture designs include the 1971 Zocker ("gambler") chair or Sitzgerat ("sitting apparatus"), which began as a child's chair and also developed into an adult's chair that fits the body and can be straddled so that the backrest becomes a table.

The Dane **Verner Panton** was perhaps more adventurous, using injection-molded plastic to create a single-piece cantilevered stacking chair. He used metal for the base of his ground-breaking Cone chair.

When **Arne Jacobsen** was asked to design the Radisson SAS Hotel in Copenhagen, the Danish architect designed furnishings as well as the building. Among these designs was the Egg chair, which used a new, innovative production technique from Norway—steam-molding polystyrene beads on to a fiberglass base; the beads became a foam in the heat from the steam. The foam was pliable and, once shaped, could be covered with boldly colored upholstery.

George Nelson's Marshmallow sofa also relies on brightly colored foam-rubber cushions for its eye-catching appeal. It was one of the first Pop Art furniture design and consisted of 18 circular cushions that appear to float above a metal frame. It was introduced in 1956 but did not prove popular with buyers—possibly because of its revolutionary design—and was taken out of production by Herman Miller, where Nelson was head of design, in 1965. **Warren Platner**'s lightweight wire furniture was also upholstered in this way.

After the gloom of the war years, consumers were avid for colorful designs.

If you want something that has great style and screams the period, look no further than these **Marcello Fantoni** 1950s faience figures. They depict Venetian revelers in the Cubist style and are covered in bright polychrome glazes. 15in (38cm) high ★ ★ ☆ ☆ ☆ ☆

The Bird chair and ottoman were part of **Harry Bertoia**'s 1952 collection of bent-steel furniture for Knoll (*below right*). The pieces are an astounding study in space, form, and function. Chair 40.25in (102cm) high ★ ★ ☆ ☆ ☆ ☆ ☆ ☆

In this Shelter Island home with fascinating textured walls and Cubist carpet, the **Warren Platner** chairs, designed for Knoll in 1966, are given a modern twist by alternating the colors of the upholstery and pillows (*opposite*).

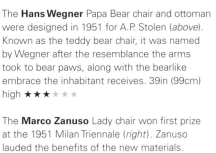

Influential pieces

Innovative designers were inspired to create chairs that fast became modern classics. Molded fiberglass and plastic could be used to create unusual shapes that offered style and comfort, enhanced by foam upholstery. The fabrics and plastics were produced in an array of bright colors that added to the eye-catching finish. While the designers experimented with these new materials, many pieces contained elements of traditional furniture—whether wing chairs (**Hans Wegner**'s Papa Bear chair and **Arne Jacobsen**'s Egg chair), French bèrgeres (**Marco Zanuso**'s Lady Chair), formal sofas (**George Nelson**'s Marshmallow sofa and **Arne Jacobsen**'s Swan sofa), or **Luigi Colani**'s daybed. These pieces were mass produced, allowing an increasing number of fashion-conscious homeowners to buy the latest trends, which still inspire designers today.

The **Hans Wegner** Papa Bear chair and ottoman were designed in 1951 for A.P. Stolen (*above*). Known as the teddy bear chair, it was named by Wegner after the resemblance the arms took to bear paws, along with the bearlike embrace the inhabitant receives. 39in (99cm) high ★★★ ★ ★ ★

The **Marco Zanuso** Lady chair won first prize at the 1951 Milan Triennale (*right*). Zanuso lauded the benefits of the new materials. 30.5in (78cm) high ★★ ★ ★ ★ ★

A TV-relax recliner by **Luigi Colani**, designed in 1967, of organically formed foam rubber upholstered in green stretch fabric. 71in (180cm) long ★ ★ ★ ★ ★

A vintage **George Nelson** and **Irving Harper** Marshmallow sofa, designed in 1956 for Herman Miller, with 18 circular cushions upholstered in original forest-green naugahyde mounted on a tubular-steel frame. 51in (129.5cm) wide ★★★☆☆

An **Arne Jacobsen** Swan sofa with royal-blue wool upholstery, on an aluminum trestle base with matte finish, with Fritz Hansen label (*above*). It was designed in 1958 and has been in production ever since. 57in (142.5cm) high ★★☆☆☆

A **George Nelson** Coconut lounge chair, designed in 1955 for, and produced by, Hermann Miller. Raised on a bent-steel, three-legged base (with nylon glides), its plastic shell seat is inspired by the shape of a slice of coconut and upholstered with a woven fabric (here coral-colored) or leather-covered one-piece foam rubber cushion. 33in (83.75cm) high ★★☆☆☆

In this classically proportioned room with its elegant period marble fireplace, the Ox or Bull chair designed by **Arne Jacobsen** dominates the space (*opposite*). It is such a strong shape that it takes no prisoners. You notice it first.

The Egg chair and ottoman were originally produced for the Radisson SAS Hotel in Copenhagen, but it soon became clear that there was a vast array of customers wanting to buy them for their homes (*this page*). The success of the Egg, and of the Swan, is their strikingly organic upholstered seats on slender cast-aluminum bases. They look cocoonlike. In this room the chair and collection of glass immediately convey that 1960s/'70s style.

Verner Panton

Heart Cone 1959

Born in Copenhagen in 1926, **Verner Panton** was educated at the Royal Danish Academy of Fine Arts and went on to become, prior to his death in 1998, one of the most experimental, innovative and influential designers of the 20th century. Stylistically, his work falls under the broad banner of Mid-Century Scandinavian Modernism. However, unlike many Scandinavian designers working during that era, Panton went beyond the use of traditional organic materials such as wood to "soften" or "humanize" the hitherto unembellished, form-strictly-follows-function designs of Modernism. Instead, and despite the fact that he didn't eschew the use of wood—notably employed in his single-form plywood S chair of 1956—Panton heartily embraced new, man-made materials. Moreover, he wasn't averse to not strictly functional, sometimes metaphoric flourishes in a design that, together with his advocacy of bright or vivid colors for interiors, played a significant role in ushering in and celebrating the Pop Art style of the 1960s.

These qualities are most readily discernible in three of Panton's most innovative designs, each of which is for a chair, and all of which have become emblems of mid-20th-century style. The Panton chair was the last of these to be designed—from the prototypes in 1960, to its official launch in 1967—but in technical terms it really was a first: namely, the first cantilevered, single-piece, injection-molded plastic chair. A sinuous S-shape in profile, easily stackable, and produced over the years in colors ranging from white to red, yellow, tangerine, and chartreuse, to ice-gray and black, it was a technical triumph, an eminently functional and comfortable chair, and a Pop Art sculpture rolled into one … and one also considered sufficiently futuristic to be featured in Stanley Kubrick's visionary 1968 film *2001: A Space Odyssey*.

In some respects, one of the chairs that preceded the Panton—the Cone, in 1958—was even more futuristic. Constructed in the sleek, fluid shape of a classic geometric cone from upholstered, thin sheet steel, it was raised on a low-profile quadruped steel base that gave it an almost gravity-defying appearance.

Its immediate successor—the third in this great triumvirate of chairs—emerged a year later, in 1959. A variation on the Cone, and equally colorful, it derived its name—the Heart or Heart Cone—from its heart-shaped silhouette, created by giving the backrest extended wings. Were they a modern development of the traditional wingback chair, or were they Mickey Mouse ears? Either way, this witty conceptual ambiguity was not only early Pop Art, but also prescient, when combined with Panton's technical ingenuity, of strands of Post Modern design.

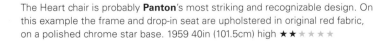

The Heart chair is probably **Panton**'s most striking and recognizable design. On this example the frame and drop-in seat are upholstered in original red fabric, on a polished chrome star base. 1959 40in (101.5cm) high ★★ ☆ ☆ ☆ ☆

In this brightly colored room with its dramatic carpet, the Heart can hold its own. The strong shape and vibrant color have made it an international success.

Piero Fornasetti

A painter, sculptor, craftsman, and decorator, **Piero Fornasetti** (1913–88) lived most of his life in Milan. His style was original and idiosyncratic, but was mainly influenced by the Neo-Classical Novecento style, and was reminiscent of Greek and Roman architecture, by which he was heavily influenced. He has become known as "the master illusionist of design." During the course of his life he designed over 13,000 objects, many of which are still in production. His witty, imaginative and boldly graphic black-and-white ceramics and furniture ranged from coasters to screens, and included quirky and fanciful ornamental umbrella stands, trays, chairs, and porcelain. The desire to create a "total design," to create a theatrical, magical space, is central to Fornasetti's work.

Many of his creations feature the face of operatic soprano Lina Cavalieri. Fornasetti found her in a 19th-century magazine. "What inspired me to create more than 500 variations on the face of a woman?" asks Fornasetti of himself. "'I don't know. I began to make them and I never stopped." The Tema e Variazioni ("theme and variations") plate series based on Cavalieri's face numbered more than 350.

In 1933 Fornasetti showed work at the Milan Triennale, including painted silk scarves, which attracted the notice of the designer **Gio Ponti.** In 1952, they collaborated on the interiors of the transatlantic liner *Andrea Dori*. One of their most important joint projects was the Architetturi line of furniture designed by Ponti and decorated with architectural quotations by Fornasetti. They showed this furniture at the 1951 Triennale. The furniture designed by Fornasetti was often decorated with trompe-l'oeil paintings of musical instruments, large suns, moons, playing cards, and animals. Fornasetti often refused to sign his work, as he regarded it as manufactured pieces, not art.

One of Fornasetti's favorite objects was the screen, with its function as a moveable architectural element. It is intrinsically theatrical and ideally suited for illusionistic tricks: "I have designed [screens] with endless motifs, but they are mostly a way of enabling me to recount some of my dreams … with its precious blue, a night sky refines the imagination so the dream remains an object, a piece of furniture …"

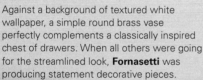

Against a background of textured white wallpaper, a simple round brass vase perfectly complements a classically inspired chest of drawers. When all others were going for the streamlined look, **Fornasetti** was producing statement decorative pieces.

A set of earthenware Buonanotte vases, designed in the 1960s, manufactured by Bitossi. The plaster prototypes were found at the beginning of the 2000s, and these were produced in 2007. 11.5in (29cm) high ★★ ★ ★ ★ ★

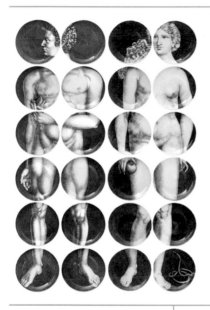

A mid- to late 20th-century set of 24 Italian Fornasetti Adam and Eve pattern porcelain plates, with transfer-printed decoration of Adam and Eve depicted across the plates. 10.25in (26cm) diam. ★★ ★ ★ ★ ★

A bureau bookcase (trumeau) "architettura" by **Piero Fornasetti** and **Gio Ponti**, decorated with black printed architectural scene on cream ground, transparent lacquer, wood and metal. c.1950 87in (218cm) high ★★★ ★ ★ ★

This chair references traditional lyre-backs, but there is no doubt that it is mid-20th century. 37in (94cm) high ★★ ★ ★ ★ ★

Fornasetti chairs have become very desirable. The Corinthian Capital was designed c.1955; this example is from 1992. 36.5in (92.5cm) high ★★ ★ ★ ★ ★

A four-panel screen decorated with hot-air balloons, on casters. As a room-divider this would be a bold decorative declaration. 19.75in (50cm) high ★★ ★ ★ ★ ★

In the living room of what used to be his home and studio in Milan (and where his son now lives), the Italian designer Piero Fornasetti re-created a Wunderkammer, a "chamber of wonders," through the use of rich, saturated colors, diverse artifacts and, of course, printed Fornasetti motifs and imagery of essentially Classical inspiration (*left*).

A **Fornasetti**-inspired rug with his signature "eye" decoration brings a classical aspect to this room, mirrored by the classical marble fireplace (*above*). Fornasetti was obsessed with eyes, and used them on his seminal collection of wall plates, Tema e Variazioni. They were inspired by the opera singer Lina Cavalieri and are both classically influenced and modern. The deep red of the rug accents the walls, which are painted a deep Caribbean blue.

Influential glass

Designers around the world used traditional techniques to create modern pieces that suited the demand for colorful glass. In Italy **Alessandro Pianon** created artist's versions of the glass novelties made for the tourist trade, while **Dino Martens** enlarged the traditional millefiori inclusions and fused them onto jugs and vases made from a patchwork of differently colored glass. **Helena Tynell** was among the Scandinavian artists who eschewed the restrained palette inspired by the natural world and used bold colors and mold-blown glass to create pieces that mimicked affordable plastic. **Winslow Anderson** and **Wayne Husted** at Blenko in the United States created large, dramatic pieces that suited the new interiors.

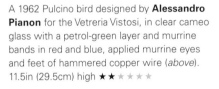

A 1962 Pulcino bird designed by **Alessandro Pianon** for the Vetreria Vistosi, in clear cameo glass with a petrol-green layer and murrine bands in red and blue, applied murrine eyes and feet of hammered copper wire (*above*). 11.5in (29.5cm) high ★★ ★ ★ ★ ★

An early 1970s ruby-red cased-glass Emma vase from the Vanha Kartano ("Country House") series designed by **Helena Tynell** for Riihimaen Lasi Oy (*right*). 8.25in (21cm) high ★ ★ ★ ★ ★ ★

An early 1950s Oriente vase designed by **Dino Martens** for the Murano glassworks Aureliano Toso (*right*). 8.25in (21cm) high ★★ ★ ★ ★ ★

A collection of colored glass vessels—primarily carafes and stoppered decanters, in diverse western and eastern styles—from not only the Italian glassmakers of Murano, but also the North American Blenko glassworks, established in 1922 in Milton, West Virginia, by **William John Blenko**.

A Blenko decanter, shape no. 6212, in turquoise glass, with a footed, onion-shaped body and an elongated teardrop stopper (*far left*). It was designed in 1961 for production from 1962 by the then chief resident designer at Blenko, **Wayne Husted**. 21.5in (52cm) high ★ ★ ★ ★ ★

A c.1970 Blenko decanter, shape no. 920 in ruby glass, with conical body and a teardrop stopper (*center*). 16in (41cm) high ★ ★ ★ ★ ★

A 1960s Blenko orange crackle glass decanter of club form with a teardrop stopper (*left*). 12.25in (31cm) high ★ ★ ★ ★ ★

Murano

Glassmaking in Murano, near Venice, underwent a transformation in the mid-20th century. Fine artists, architects and sculptors were taken on as designers. Many were freelance, so worked at different factories during their careers. Some companies, such as Venini, even employed designers from outside Italy, with that company bringing in the talents of key designers from Scandinavian countries. This injected Murano glass with a very different aesthetic. Colors erupted in a rainbow of vibrancy, and were often contrasted with one another. Forms also changed. The fussy complexity of historical forms was abandoned, to be replaced by simple, clean-lined shapes. Some designs, such as those produced by **Ercole Barovier**, consciously echoed historic and traditional designs, but updated them in a strongly modern idiom.

In the interiors of the period, the cheerfully colored, often whimsical, pieces matched perfectly the modern furniture designs being produced across Europe and the U.S. New factories were set up in this period, including Cenedese and Vistosi. At Seguso, **Flavio Poli** perfected the sommerso technique, where layers of different colored glass create organic forms.

The success inspired smaller, less well-known factories on Murano to copy the work of the leading designers. Typically smaller, lower-quality imitations flooded the market and were exported all over the world as inexpensive ornaments for modern interiors, or were sold to tourists as souvenirs of the island.

The groundbreaking work of these far-sighted designers, combined with the enormous output of the industry they inspired, put Murano glass firmly at the forefront of European glass design by the late 1950s. This was built on over the following decades to the extent that the descriptive term "Murano glass" almost became a hotly desirable "brand" across the world during the late 20th century. This is a fertile area for vintage collectors, as many of these Mid-Century Modern pieces of glass appear at fairs, auctions, and for sale online.

A diverse collection of Mid-Century Murano colored glass is displayed on this drop-end table. Typical Muranese decorative techniques on display in these vessels include murrines, filigrana, sommerso, and aventurine inclusions.

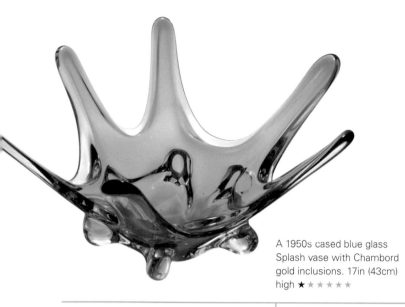

A 1950s cased blue glass Splash vase with Chambord gold inclusions. 17in (43cm) high ★ ★ ★ ★ ★ ★

An early 1950s Pezzato Parigi glass vase by **Fulvio Bianconi** for the Venini glassworks, its clear-glass body overlaid with polychrome tesserae. 9in (22.5cm) high ★ ★ ★ ★ ★ ★

An early 1950s oriente vase by **Dino Martens** for Fratelli Toso. 11in (28cm) high ★ ★ ★ ★ ★ ★

An early 1950s stellato vase by **Pollio Perelda** for Fratelli Toso. 11in (28.5cm) high ★ ★ ★ ★ ★ ★

A late 1950s cased-glass vase by **Anzolo Fuga** for AVEM. 9.25in (25cm) high ★ ★ ★ ★ ★ ★

An early 1960s Barovier & Toso disc-handled, teardrop-shape, brown glass vase on oval stand, its vertical ribbing with aventurine and white band decoration. 11.25in (28cm) high ★ ★ ★ ★ ★ ★

A mid-1960s sommerso glass fish on matching plinth, a translucent colored glass cased within colorless glass form designed by **Antonio Da Ros** for Fratelli Cenedese. 12.5in (32cm) high ★ ★ ★ ★ ★ ★

Fun Ceramics
Post-war optimism brought with it a new domesticity in which entertaining at home became increasingly popular. Many potteries began to mass-produce dinner services that reflected the fashions of the time. British potteries commissioned designers to bring up-to-the-minute designs to their tablewares. At the Midwinter Pottery, **Jessie Tait**'s designs included the floral Primavera and zebra-striped Zambesi. Art pottery took two forms: plates and other vessels decorated by artists such as Pablo Picasso and Jean Cocteau, and hand-decorated mass-produced vases from West German potteries such as Scheurich and Bay Keramik. These pieces have become known as "fat lava" thanks to the thick, bubbled glazes.

A 1950s Lenci pottery jug of stylized bird-like form, with hand-painted polychrome decoration (*above*). 11.75in (30cm) high
★ ★ ★ ★

A late 1950s/early 1960s "Edition originale de Jean Cocteau" red clay charger from the Madeline-Jolly pottery, hand-painted with flute-playing Pan (*top right*). 12in (30.5cm) diam. ★ ★ ★ ★ ★ ★

A 1950s Midwinter Pottery Stylecraft shape meat plate with hand-painted Primavera pattern, designed by **Jessie Tait** (*above right*). 14in (35.5cm) wide ★ ★ ★ ★ ★ ★

A 1970s Roth Keramik no. 312 vase with orange gloss and black "fat lava" glazes (*right*). 12in (30.5cm) high ★ ★ ★ ★ ★ ★

A late 1960s Poole Pottery carved Delphis vase, hand-painted by **Irene Kirton** (*far right*). 15.5in (39.5cm) high ★ ★ ★ ★ ★ ★

Czech Glass

Cut off from the west by the Iron Curtain after World War II, Czech designers were charged with showing the success of the new Communist regime through their designs, while raising foreign currency by making pieces for export. The creativity of the designers was boosted because their government did not believe glass could carry a political or social message. They were subject to fewer controls than other artists, and were free to create as they chose. For example, glass by **Jan Kotik** shows an abstract style that would have been banned if used in another medium.

Some of the most forward-thinking and unusual designs were made by **Pavel Hlava**, **Jiří Harcuba**, **Stanislav Libensky**, and **René Roubíček**. Many of them won awards at major international exhibitions, including the 1957 Milan Triennale and 1958 Brussels Exposition. Essentially, they made two sorts of design: unique pieces or limited editions of experimental glass, and mass-produced designs inspired by them and sold to an international clientele.

Many pieces by names such as **Jan Beranek**, **Frantisek Zemek**, and **Jaroslav Beranek** are sculptural, curved forms that made the most of the plastic nature of glass. Designers including **Josef Hospodka** for Chribska and **Milan Metelak** for Harochov used bright colors for their designs that can be mistaken for pieces from Murano (it is possible they were inspired by pieces from Italian glassworks). Glass with a Scandinavian feel, with cool colors and straight lines, was made by **Miloslav Klinger** for Zelezny Brod. Other designers, such as **Josef Svarc**, **Josef Pravec**, **Vladimir Zahour**, and **Ladislav Oliva**, used the traditional glass-cutting techniques Czech glassworks were renowned for to create modern pieces. Some used lens, prismatic and other optical cuts that made the most of the reflective qualities of glass, while others created stylized naturalistic or figurative motifs. Enamels and gilding were also used on glass to create abstract, geometric, or stylized floral patterns. Most of this glass was hand-blown and -decorated, but some pieces were mass-produced from pressed glass.

The names of these designers were virtually unknown before the Velvet Revolution of 1989, after which they and their designs began to be re-evaluated.

A 1960s rose-pink, green and colorless cased-glass vase no.5968 from the Czechoslovakian Skrdlovice (originally Beranek) glassworks, designed in 1959 by **Jan Beranek**, son of a co-founder of the company. One of Skrdlovice's best-known designs, with its distinctive pulled wavelike swirls, this vase was produced in many different colorways, including purple, blue, and uranium green. 12in (30.5cm) high ★ ★ ★ ★ ★

A 1960s elliptical glass bowl from the Czechoslovakian Mstisov glassworks, and designed in 1959 by **Frantisek Zemek** (above). From the Murano-like Harmony range, it is typical of Zemek's asymmetric, organic forms and features blue-glass trails over a colorless cased green body. 11.5in (29.5cm) high ★ ★ ★ ★ ★

A 1960s blue, green and colorless cased-glass vase no. 5346 (above). Of diagonally spiraling or twisted ropelike form, it is from the Skrdlovice glassworks' Andromeda range, and was originally designed by **Jaroslav Beranek** in 1953. 12in (30.5cm) high ★ ★ ★ ★ ★

A 1970s amber-glass vase no. 40114 with applied blue-green prunts impressed with a grid pattern. Made by the Czech Prachen glassworks, it was designed by **Josef Hospodka** in 1969. 12.5in (32cm) high ★ ★ ★ ★ ★

Colorful living

The 1950s arrived with more than a splash of color. Furniture was designed to appear light and airy, with thin steel rods providing minimal yet sturdy support. Chairs, in particular, were designed for comfort and to suit a more relaxed way of living.

Modern homes were built with large windows to let in the light. This was enhanced by walls painted white or in pale, neutral colors and decorated with bold paintings and wall-hangings. Further contrast might be supplied by boldly colored rugs and carpets on the floors. Color schemes often echoed the soft, naturalistic shades favored by Scandinavian designers, or the bright, bold hues seen in Murano glass. In many ways they presaged the Pop movement of the 1960s and '70s that introduced bright, clashing colors to every aspect of life—from fashionable clothing to decorations in the home.

Semi-opaque sliding screens open and close access to this library-walled den, while slightly raised and contrasting-colored wooden flooring helps to define the area when they are open (*below*). An inviting space is made more so by the inclusion of **Eero Saarinen**'s supremely comfortable mid- to late 1940s Womb chair and matching ottoman.

The rectilinear forms of a pair of blue vinyl-upholstered slipper chairs echo the clarity of line and, above all, elegance of Art Deco predecessors (*opposite*).

Bright-blue curtains, a mustard-yellow sideboard, and a sky-blue RAR rocker (designed in 1948–50 by **Charles** and **Ray Eames**) provide bold and vibrant contrasts of color with an essentially white decorative ground.

Hot carpet, hot sofas, and chairs (designed by
Jim Isermann and **Carol Vena-Mondt**), and
possibly hot-house flowers burn even brighter
against white walls.

Stealing the show from an array of artwork, an elliptical **Charles** and **Ray Eames** coffee table, an **Eero Saarinen** Womb chair and matching ottoman, and a **Mies van der Rohe** Barcelona ottoman is a deep shag-pile carpet, color-coordinated in black, white, and gray, and an upholstered modular sofa (*above*).

Mid- to late 19th-century Victorian style, in the form of a cast-iron fire surround, hood, and grate, meets Mid-Century Modern, in the form of **Eero Saarinen**'s fiberglass, aluminum and plastic Tulip chairs and marble-topped table (*right*).

In a bright Amsterdam kitchen, the strong contrasts of materials, form and style between on the one hand high-gloss white laminated cabinetry, and a white fiberglass and plastic **Eames** DSR chair with a chromed-metal "Eiffel Tower" base, and on the other hand a 19th-century mahogany, tripod-base, circular breakfast table and a traditional wooden artist's easel are boldly unified by the use of strong and contrasting color, in the form of a pink backsplash and seat-pad, and a sand- and sienna-dyed rug (*opposite*).

In a well-lit living area, the overtly rectilinear qualities of a pair of red upholstered matching sofas and a white coffee table are both augmented and softened by the inclusion of a pair of classic bent-tubular-steel and brown-leather Wassily B3 armchairs, designed in 1926 by Bauhaus student and then teacher **Marcel Breuer**, and subsequently named after the abstract painter Wassily Kandinsky, who had particularly admired them while also teaching there (*left*).

Set against a monumental natural stone wall and raised on stainless-steel legs with disc feet, Brueton's three-seater, leather-upholstered Undulatus bench, designed by **Stanley Jay Friedman**, presents as both sculpture and seating (*below*).

Hovering above a contemporary dining table and dining chairs with stained red wooden seats and backrests is American designer **George Nelson**'s iconic vinyl-covered, wire-framed, saucer pendant Bubble lamp, designed in 1947 and first produced by Herman Miller in 1952 (*opposite*).

POP AND SPACE AGE

The late 1950s saw a revolution in design that brought eye-catching, futuristic design to the home. The Pop Art movement—a reaction against the establishment—aimed to connect art to ordinary lives. Bright colors and innovative shapes were used to create novel, cheap, disposable objects, many of them made from paper or plastic. At the same time, advances in science and the space race brought shapes and textures into the home that many considered to be out of this world. Televisions shaped like spacemen's helmets and clocks with atom balls in place of the numerals were among the furnishings being developed.

opposite, clockwise from top left A Space Age folly lands in rural Normandy. Conceived in concrete and glass, it was built in 1973–76, having been commissioned by the son of a wealthy builder who had returned from several inspirational months in San Francisco. / Created with silvered acrylic bubbles, large screens draw on both Op Art and Space Age aesthetics to stimulate reflections and distortions of both light and space. / Texture was often as important as pattern and color in 1950s and '60s interiors. Here John Barman has contrasted not only patterned red "solid" black and white, but also the smoothness of steel with the rough and raised textures of, respectively, the chair cover and the carpet.

right Here, too, contrasts of texture are just as important as contrasts of color in defining both the architectural features and the overall space. The smooth floor is painted white; the curved outer walls carpeted off-white; the curved inner wall in earth-brown-and-black tiles in high relief; and the undulating ceiling draped in orange-red jersey.

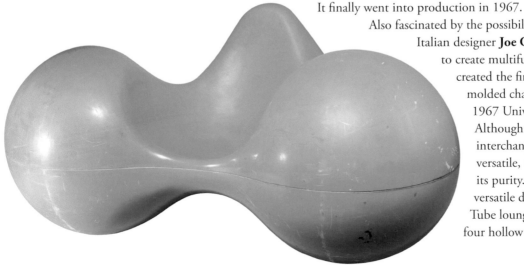

An acrylic-bodied, steel-framed and suspended Bubble chair, a 1968 development by **Eero Aarnio** of his 1963 Ball chair. 44.75in (113.5cm) diameter ★ ★ ☆ ☆ ☆ ☆

A brave new world

In the 1960s designers who had pushed the possibilities of traditional materials as far as they could started to look to plastics and other new materials to create sensational new furnishings. The organic shapes and bright colors they used were inspired by—and helped to make possible—a new, relaxed way of living and were in tune with the new Pop Art movement. Many were also inspired by the new Space Age, which had the public enthralled.

Fiberglass-reinforced plastic made it possible to construct a chair seat and back in one piece. In 1950 the American designers **Charles** and **Ray Eames** were the first to produce a range of mass-produced plastic chairs using this material, many supported by metal-rod bases. As well as stacking chairs, it included the RAR (Rocking Armchair Rod chair) and LAR (Lounge Arm Rod chair).

Finnish designer **Eero Aarnio**'s Ball chair—designed in 1963—is a prime example of the New Look: a hollow sphere with a slice removed and set on a circular swivel base. Made from fiberglass-reinforced plastic, it was durable and waterproof, so it could be used inside and out. It was made in a selection of colors (originally black, white, orange, and red) and could be customized to make it a room within a room. Speakers could be added to the upholstered interior to make it the perfect cocoon in which to listen to the latest cool sounds, or the owner could curl up inside to talk on the telephone.

Aarnio's designs included the Pastil chair (1967), which was inspired by a simple sweet. His 1971 Tomato chair was designed to be an improvement on the Pastil. He explains: "I realized that Pastil chair floats and carries the person who sits in it in water but it is very rickety. If there were three items like two great armrests and the back of the chair it would be stable, and this is how the idea of the Tomato chair was born. The name reflects its looks: looking at the chair from the front there are two round shapes, i.e. two circles like in the word tOmatO."

In 1956 **Verner Panton** designed the S chair, which took the possibilities of molded plywood to the limit. The organic, cantilevered shape was designed to fit the human body and inspired many designers to follow in his footsteps. Three years later the Danish designer used similar principles for the prototype of his stacking side chair, which was made from injection-molded plastic. It finally went into production in 1967.

Also fascinated by the possibilities of plastic was the Italian designer **Joe Colombo**. He used it to create multifunctional designs. He created the first full-size injection-molded chair on the market—the 1967 Universale 4860 chair. Although its detachable and interchangeable legs made it versatile, the design lost some of its purity. Typical of his functional, versatile designs are the 1969 Tube lounger, which consists of four hollow cylinders that can be

Eero Aarnio's sculptural Tomato chair comprises three primarily globular forms—two for the arms, one for the back—and an additional semi-globe for the seat, molded from polyester and fiberglass, and designed in 1971. 55in (140cm) wide ★ ★ ☆ ☆ ☆ ☆

Verner Panton's revolutionary single-form, lacquered-plywood S chair was developed in 1956, and was a forerunner of his similar and even more iconic injection-molded plastic Panton chair, developed 1959–67. 32.75in (83cm) high ★★★★★★

Charles and **Ray Eames**'s RAR (Rocking Armchair Rod) chair is one of a number of revolutionary molded, fiberglass-reinforced plastic chairs with metal-rod bases they developed c.1948–50; others include the DAR, DSR, and LAR. 26.5in (67cm) high ★★★★★★

Joe Colombo's one-piece, injection-molded, colored-plastic Universal chair was designed in 1965–67, and originally manufactured by Kartell, in Italy. 28.5in (72.5cm) high ★★★★★★ new ★★★★★★ for an original

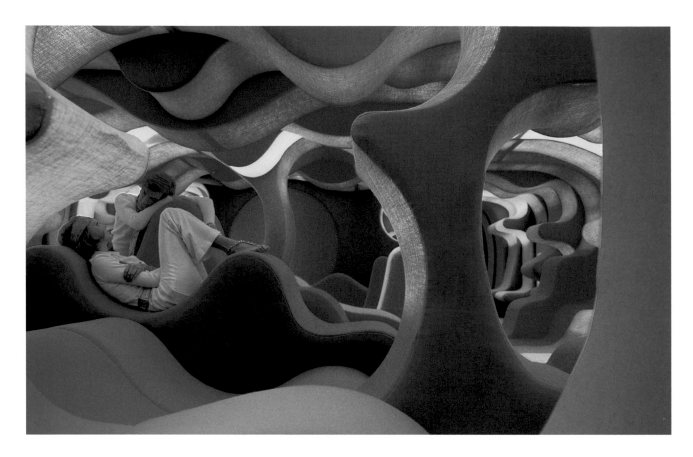

Built on the pleasure boat the Bayer chemical company rented during the Cologne Furniture Fair, and intended to promote the use of synthetic materials in home furnishings, Visona 2 was designed by **Verner Panton** in 1970. It remains not only a hugely innovative take on Organic Modern and Space Age design, but also one of the 20th century's most spectacular examples of installation art.

Living Tower seating, in orange, designed in 1970 by **Verner Panton** and manufactured by Vitra. 78.5in (200cm) wide ★ ★ ☆ ☆ ☆ ☆

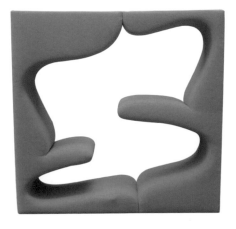

attached in any configuration. Colombo also designed lighting and was fascinated by storage furniture. His Boby storage trolley, a wheeled cabinet with rotating drawers, has been a best-seller since its arrival in 1970.

The possibilities molded plastics brought to lighting were endless, and such objects proved to be less expensive to produce than those in traditional lighting materials such as metal and glass. Verner Panton turned his attention to lighting and used simple forms to create maximum light. His 1968 Flower Pot hanging lamp consists of two half spheres, one half the size of the other. The small, lower sphere hides the bulb and its interior reflects light into the surface of the larger sphere above it. For the Visona 2 exhibition at the 1970 Cologne Furniture Fair Panton adapted his earlier Fun lamps, which consisted of a series of translucent shell discs suspended from a metal ring and surrounding the bulb, to use colored or chrome-plated plastic balls. The Type H Ball lamp features balls of equal size in a spherical formation; in others, balls of different sizes were arranged on strings.

The new consumer dream promoted throwaway products and encouraged people to buy the latest items by famous designers. This extended to technology and other furnishings: televisions, telephones, clocks, and textiles.

The dawn of the atomic age inspired designers to use scientific forms in their work. **George Nelson**'s Ball clock, designed for the American Howard Miller Clock Company in 1947, was based on atomic structures.

The American lunar landing in 1969 also had an effect on design. The JVC Videosphere television, which arrived on the market in the same year, was based on the spacemen's helmets.

In the same way that new chairs were shaped to the contours of the human body, making other consumer goods that were fit for purpose was important to many, and filtered into technological design. Ericksson's Ericfon telephone handset, designed in the late 1940s and in production from 1954, was a one-piece device designed to fit the face and with the dial in the base. Its unusual shape brought it the nickname the Cobra. Equally popular was the British Trimphone (Tone Ringer Illuminated Model), which was found in thousands of homes following its launch in 1964.

Nature also played a role in the designs of the 1950s and '60s. British textile designer **Lucienne Day**, who was married to furniture designer **Robin Day**, is credited with changing the face of British interiors with a huge range of products. Her best-known textile design, Calyx, uses stylized flowers consisting of vertical stems and semi-circular buds and was inspired by the way Scandinavian designers alluded to natural forms in their work.

Such was the universal appeal of plastic that in 1969 **Per Lütken**, designer at Denmark's Holmegaard glass factory, turned his back on the budlike curving shapes he had been designing and started to make glass that almost looked like plastic. His Carnaby range was produced in vibrant colors, including yellow, blue, and red. These were lined with opaque white glass to enhance the effect. He incorporated Pop Art geometric shapes including combinations of cylinders, discs, and spheres.

This was a period of rampant consumerism, when designers found a willing public avidly awaiting the next "new thing."

Good ergonomics—easy-to-use push-button dialing and an ear-to-mouth, head-contoured handset—underpinned the British Trimphone, shown here in turquoise and launched in 1964. 8in (20cm) long ★ ★ ★ ★ ★

Lucienne Day's Calyx fabric pattern was designed in 1951 for the Festival of Britain, and subsequently produced by Heals & Sons Ltd., London. Its plant-form imagery of grasses and flowers, rendered in a number of colorways, was inspired by the work of the artists Wassily Kandinsky and Paul Klee.

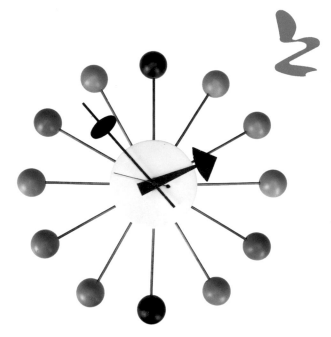

⟲ Influential pieces

A series of revolutions in the way people lived influenced designs from the late 1950s into the 1960s and '70s. The possibility of space travel inspired JVC's Videosphere television, which looked like a space helmet. The way in which the Pop Art movement challenged perceptions of art encouraged designers such as **Geoffrey Baxter** at Whitefriars to bring unusual shapes and textures to brightly colored glass. And while designers such as **George Nelson** were inspired by scientific advances to add atom balls to clock designs, **Joe Colombo**, on the other hand, aimed to create comfortable furniture, some of which could be reconfigured to suit the user.

A **George Nelson–Irving Harper** Ball clock, conceived in 1948, with enameled metal hands and, in a nod to Abstract Expressionism and radiating from brass spokes, polychrome wooden spheres in lieu of numerals (*above*). 13.25in (34cm) diam. ★ ☆ ☆ ☆ ☆ ☆ new

Conceived in 1963 and named after his wife, **Joe Colombo**'s Elda chair comprises a distinctively leather-upholstered armchair with a fiberglass-reinforced plastic shell and base (*right*). 37in (94cm) high ★★ ☆ ☆ ☆ ☆ original

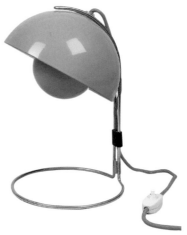

A 1970s JVC Videosphere television set in the shape of an astronaut's helmet, with a colored-plastic carcass and smoked-Perspex screen visor. 14.5in (36.75cm) high
★ ★ ★ ★ ★ ★

A Whitefriars Drunken Bricklayer vase in textured kingfisher-blue glass, designed by **Geoffrey Baxter** c.1970. 13.5in (34.5cm) high
★ ★ ★ ★ ★ ★

A Flowerpot table lamp with enameled (here orange) metal shade, designed with pendant equivalents in 1968 by **Verner Panton**. 14in (35.5cm) high ★ ★ ★ ★ ★ ★ new

Italian **Joe Colombo**'s revolutionary Tube chair combines four hollow PVC cylinders of graduated size, each upholstered in either vinyl- or leather-covered polyurethane foam. Clipped together by six steel-and-rubber-ball clips, the tubes can be configured in various combinations to suit the sitter—a functional flexibility that made the chair as useful as it was innovative. 1969 47.25in (120cm) long ★ ★ ★ ★ ★ ★ original

Danish designer **Per Lütken** worked for 56 years at the Holmegaard glassworks, and one of the most innovative commercially successful ranges he conceived for it was the Carnaby vases of the 1960s and early '70s (*left*). Named after the most fashionable street in "swinging '60s" London, they were mold-blown and cased, produced in various "exotic" shapes—cylinders and onion- and disc-shaped knops were recurring forms—and characterized by bright, vibrant colors, such as the yellow, white-under-red, and white-under-blue shown here, strongly associated with contemporary Pop Art. Largest 11.75in (30cm) high ★ ★ ★ ★ ★

Having already established a reputation for a sculptural approach to furniture design through his technique of stack-laminating wood, **Wendell Castle** turned, in 1969–70, to new and more affordable materials. The result was his gel-coated, fiberglass-reinforced plastic Molar Group range of furniture (*above*). To a contemporary public enamored with Pop Art, their toothlike forms and vibrant, candy colors (here represented in pink and yellow) proved an instant hit, and prompted Castle to employ the same materials and colors in other conceptual pieces, such as the c.1972 quadrant Puzzle table in red (*left*). Yellow molar 37in (94cm) wide NPA

A white **Wendell Castle** Molar Group chair competes for pride of place in the "Florida Room" of Doug Meyer's Miami home. Putting up stiff opposition is a pair of vintage figural Raymor lamps, a 1970s Milo Baughman sofa, a steel pedestal-mounted, Nakashima-style barkwood-topped coffee table, and a 1962 Warhol *Marilyn*.

Eero Saarinen Conference chairs and a **Verner Panton** Ball lamp feature in this red, white, and orange color-schemed dining room in a **Donald Wexler**-designed house in Palm Springs.

Celluloid balls, here in red (*above*), are hung on nylon wires from a metal ring cage in **Verner Panton**'s Type H lamp (also known as the Ball lamp or the Wonder lamp). 1969 17.25in (44cm) diameter ★★★★★★

Panton's pendant Flowerpot lamp (*right*) comprises two semi-circular spheres in stainless steel, here finished in a yellow-green pattern. 1969 19.5in (49.5cm) diameter ★★★★★★

This unattributed table lamp features an abstract-patterned shade on an inverted trumpet-form base of chromed steel wire, in the style of Verner Panton (*below*). 17in (42cm) diameter ★★★★★★

The injection-molded, thermoplastic Nesso lamp was designed by Gruppo Architetti Urbanisti Città Nuova for Artemide in 1967 (*below right*). 8.5in (21.5cm) diameter ★★★★★★

Futuristic lighting

Colorful molded plastics allowed designers to create unusual, sculptural lighting that celebrated the Pop Art movement. Many of **Verner Panton**'s lamps use spheres and hemispheres to create simple pieces that catch the attention and diffuse light around the room. He used dozens of plastic balls to create a Pop chandelier (known as the Type H dome lamp) and a large and small hemisphere that fit together to celebrate Flower Power (the Flowerpot lamp). When switched on, the translucent plastic of Artemide's Nesso lamp glows in the dark. For those who wanted pattern as well as light from a lamp, Panton and others created bold lampshade designs that sat on simple lamp bases.

Eero Aarnio

Ball chair 1963

Finnish interior and product designer **Eero Aarnio** was born in Helsinki in 1932, studied at the city's Institute of Industrial Art, and founded his own freelance practice in 1962. Exploiting cutting-edge experiments in plastics and, especially, fiberglass technology—the latter given earlier and considerable impetus by American designers **Charles** and **Ray Eames** in the 1950s—Aarnio achieved international recognition just four years later following an exhibition at the Cologne Furniture Fair of 1966. On display was a single chair, the prototype of which he had designed for his own domestic use three years earlier. Named the Ball chair (and sometimes referred to as the Globe), it caused a sensation, receiving instant critical acclaim.

Raised on a circular steel pedestal base, the fiberglass frame of the Ball is in the form of a perfect sphere from which a large slice has been cut at an oblique angle to give access to the hollow interior. Fully upholstered, including seat and back cushions, the contrasting-colored interior cocoons the sitter not only in great comfort, but also, particularly if the occupant sits well back, in near-silence, since the largely enclosed, upholstered fiberglass form cut out most exterior sounds. The overall effect is the creation of a sense of privacy and personal space that has been described as rather like sitting in "a room within a room." This is not to say, however, that the occupant is per se cut off, as the sphere can be turned on its own axis above the metal base to provide 360 degrees of outlook.

Significantly, Aarnio had installed in his prototype a red telephone. This not only contributed to the sense of personal, private space, but also reinforced the futuristic technological buzz of it all. Together with its planetary spherical shape (originally manufactured in orange, red, black, or white), this virtually guaranteed from the outset the Ball's reputation as an icon of 1960s Space Age design. Indeed, in 1968 Aarnio took the design a stage further with the Bubble chair. Of similar spherical form to the Ball, but made of transparent acrylic and suspended from the ceiling rather than raised from the floor, it conferred on an occupant both the appearance and the sensation of floating in space! Not surprisingly, the simple geometric forms of Aarnio's Space Age designs, which also included his 1971 triple-balled, fiberglass Tomato chair, were well suited to and appeared on the sets of numerous science-fiction productions—cinema and TV—in vogue in the late 1960s and early '70s. As such, they made a major contribution to the perception that fictional science future had became factual science now, a fact confirmed by the Apollo moon landings in 1969.

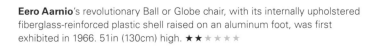

Eero Aarnio's revolutionary Ball or Globe chair, with its internally upholstered fiberglass-reinforced plastic shell raised on an aluminum foot, was first exhibited in 1966. 51in (130cm) high. ★ ★ ☆ ☆ ☆ ☆

Eero Aarnio's 1968 development of the Ball chair—the ceiling-suspended, clear-acrylic-bodied Bubble—hangs in a Kelly Hoppen sitting room.

Crazy chairs

Chair designers discovered that there were no limits to the inspiration for their work—and the ability to mold plastics into any form meant they could go in any direction they chose. Many of these designs were devised to fit the contours of the body. Some examples—**Pierre Paulin**'s Tongue chairs, **Olivier Mourgue**'s daybed, and Gruppo 14's Flocco armchair—are almost sculptural in their forms. Meanwhile Paulin's Butterfly chair is the essence of minimalism and **Jørgen Høvelskov**'s harp or string chair simply experimental. Many have become design classics. The Joe Seat was designed by **Jonathan De Pas**, **Donato D'Urbino**, and **Paolo Lomazzi** as a tribute to the baseball player Joe DiMaggio and to fit the sitter like a glove.

A pair, in orange and red, of Tongue chaise longue chairs, designed by **Pierre Paulin** for Artifort in 1967 (*above*). 33.5in (85cm) wide ★★ ☆ ☆ ☆ ☆ the pair new

Christened the Viking, but known since its launch in 1963 as the Harp, this Danish chair was designed by **Jørgen Høvelskov** (*above right*). 54in (136.5cm) high ★ ☆ ☆ ☆ ☆ ☆

The leather-upholstered Glove or Joe chair was designed in 1970 by **Jonathan De Pas**, **Donato D'Urbino** and **Paolo Lomazzi**, and dedicated to baseball legend Joe DiMaggio (*right*). 65.75in (167cm) wide ★ ★ ☆ ☆ ☆

Olivier Mourgue's Djinn Relaxer was designed for Airborne International in 1965 (*top left*). 66in (168cm) long ★★ ☆ ☆ ☆ ☆

Pierre Paulin's steel-rod-framed, leather-upholstered F675, better known as the Butterfly chair, was designed for Artifort in 1963 (*top right*). 32in (81cm) wide ★★ ☆ ☆ ☆ ☆

The Fiocco lounge chair was designed in 1970 by **Gianni Pareschi** of the Italian G14 Group for Busnelli (*above*). 47.25in (120cm) deep ★★ ☆ ☆ ☆ ☆

The Garden Egg chair, with an articulated top/backrest, was designed in 1968 by **Peter Ghyczy** for the polyurethane factory Elastogran GmbH in West Germany (*left*). 29in (74cm) wide ★★ ☆ ☆ ☆ ☆

Modern homes

Open-plan living came to the fore in the 1960s, and color, furniture, and lighting were used to create zones rather than separate rooms in these large living spaces. Large, white-walled, airy spaces were the perfect backdrop to exuberant furnishings made from the latest materials and using new technology. Colorful upholstery, white plastics, and chrome and steel supports created a truly modern look.

Large windows let in plenty of natural light, while atmospheric lighting was created by combinations of wall, ceiling, and table lamps. Mirrored surfaces might be used to reflect and refract the light.

These interiors eschewed clutter in favor of a few decorative elements that enhanced the space and complemented the rest of the room. Many of the furniture designs of the time feature large, plain, sometimes polished surfaces. Visual interest was created using sculptural forms, patterned or textured textiles, bold artwork, and textured ceilings that helped to diffuse the light.

The aim for many designers was to redefine domestic interiors and create a new, informal way of living. **Verner Panton** explained it as follows: "The main purpose of my work is to provoke people into using their imaginations. Most people spend their lives in dreary gray-beige conformity, mortally afraid of using colors. By experimenting with lighting, colors, textiles, and furniture and utilizing the latest technologies, I try to show new ways to encourage people to use their fantasy and make their surroundings more exciting."

The result would be cozy or futuristic but never dull.

In an Emmanuel Renoird-restored mid-1970s-built house in rural Normandy, France, an Arctic Peaks ceiling with concealed polychrome lighting is suspended above a similarly white interior with a polished resin floor. Furnishings accompanying the pair of present-day Alfa sofas in scarlet, by Zanotta, are a late 1950s-designed, marble-topped Tulip table by **Eero Saarinen**, and a pair of unattributed 1970s, swivel tub chairs. Star-base-mounted and yellow-upholstered, their form echoes Saarinen's Tulip chairs in an adjacent dining room.

The essence of 1970s style is captured in these two bedrooms in a 1970s-built house in Normandy, restored by Emmanuel Renoird. In the master bedroom (*above*) an oval French bed is flanked by a pair of **Eero Saarinen** pedestal-footed side tables with form-echoing lamps, the latter in white echoing the walls and ceiling. Decade-characteristic splashes of color are present in an Italian orange Plexiglas armchair from the1960s, in the shades of blue and purple artwork, in a red radiator-hiding screen and, through the door, in one of Andy Warhol's iconic pictures of Marilyn Monroe. In the guest bedroom (*left*) a polychrome geometric painting by Geneviève Gleize also hangs on white walls above a bed with a white molded-polyester frame, designed by **Marc Held** for Prisunic in 1970; on it, the biggest splash of color is provided by a Lapin Rouge bedcover designed by Renoird.

Soft-sheen black walls and a black carpet are counterbalanced by not only a white ottoman, but also an abundance of natural light and views and a substantial view of Manhattan (*opposite*). Splashes of warm color are introduced in the pair of reverse-cantilevered, yellow-green upholstered armchairs with red shag-pile scatter pillows.

Orange, from the yellowest to the reddest shades, was a recurring hue in mid-1960s to mid-1970s color schemes. Strongly contrasted with white walls, it is employed to impressive effect in geometric-pattern bedding and one of the two **George Nelson**-designed Vitra wall-hung Ball clocks in this bedroom (*above*). In a paler, yellower shade, it is used equally dramatically as a solid, rather than patterned, block of contrasting-with-white color on the headboard, oval frame, and fabric cover of a bed (*left*). Perhaps most innovative of all, however, is its conspicuous deployment behind a white-framed panel of downlighters in the winter garden terrace (*opposite*). The enameled decoration of the tubular frames of the 1927-designed MR10 and MR20 chairs by **Ludwig Mies van der Rohe** serves to enhance the impact.

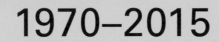

NEW MODERNS

1970–2015

The final decades of the 20th century and the first years of the new millennium saw design explode in every direction, embracing the radical, and both rejecting and celebrating what had gone before.

Craig Morrison's Sticky Marshmallow sofa uses latex to push the boundaries of furniture design.
c.2000 62.5in (159cm) high ★★ ★ ★ ★

An Anarchy of Styles

As the 1970s began, many designers felt Modernism had had its day and it was time to look for new inspiration. They rejected the idea that "form follows function" and instead created designs that made a statement rather than improved their surroundings. The result was a clash of styles, materials, and methods used to create colorful, outrageous pieces. The best of these Post Modern pieces were probably made by Studio Alchimia and the Memphis design group in Milan, but their reign was short. By the early 1980s designers were returning to the uncluttered lines that became Minimalism, and furniture made from recycled materials that satisfied a need to protect the planet.

Wendell Castle was inspired by Abstract Expressionism when he designed this Caligari piano and bench for Steinway & Sons. The case is painted with loose indigo brushstrokes on a white background. 1990 69.75in (177.5cm) wide ★★★★★ ☆

The anthropomorphic legs on his Juicy Salif juicer are typical of **Philippe Starck**'s work. Designed in 1990 for Alessi, it is made of cast aluminum with polyamide feet. 11.5in (29cm) high ★ ☆ ☆ ☆ ☆ ☆

The whimsical nature of **Pedro Friedeberg**'s work can be seen in this three-legged figural mahogany clock painted in red and gold. The battery movement is in a hinged panel in the back leg. 23in (58cm) high ★★ ☆ ☆ ☆ ☆

Michael Graves designed Classical details such as busts set on faux marble plinths for this living room (*opposite*). The exaggerated armchairs and mirrored ceiling add to the playful effect.

Shaped like oversized pills, **Cesare Casati** and **Emanuele Ponzio**'s Pillola floor lamps sit on plastic bases and can be angled to different directions (*above*). The plastic lamps were manufactured by Ponteur, Italy. 1968 21.5in (55cm) high ★★ ★ ★ ★ ★

In contrast to the pared-down aesthetic of this library, with its white walls and functional lighting, **Alessandro Mendini**'s Proust armchair by Capellini makes a dramatic statement and a cozy place to read (*opposite*).

The seat and exaggerated cylindrical back rest/bolster of **Shiro Kuramata**'s Sofa with Arms chair appear to float above the ground, while the tubular-steel frame is a pastiche of 1920s Modernist designs and also references **Ettore Sottsass**'s work from the late 1970s and early 1980s (*below*). 1982 24.5in (62.5cm) wide ★★★ ★ ★ ★

The Modernist designs of the 1930s and '40s were reinterpreted during the 1950s and '60s to bring a more human element to interiors. As the heady days of the 1960s gave way to economic uncertainly in the mid-1970s, this gradual change was not enough and designers looked for something new—radically new.

The result became known as Post Modernism, and it combined everything Modernist designers had rejected. Work by people such as **Ettore Sottsass**, **Alessandro Mendini**, and **Michael Graves** combined wood and plastic, the latest technology with traditional woodworking techniques, and new and ancient forms into colorful pieces. Their manifesto can best be summed up by Sottsass when he said: "I believe that the future only begins when the past has been completely dismantled, its logic reduced to dust and nostalgia is all that remains." The American architect **Robert Venturi** put it more succinctly when he responded to **Ludwig Mies van der Rohe**'s dictum "less is more" by declaring that "less is a bore."

For many, Post Modernism is a chaotic jumble of ideas best seen in the work of Milan's Studio Alchimia and Memphis design group. Studio Alchimia, led by architect and designer Alessandro Mendini, was never a commercial success, but its influence was widespread and it paved the way for Memphis.

Memphis was led by Sottsass. He named this witty and irreverent look the New International Style and it caused a sensation when it was launched in 1981. Among the international designers who worked with him were Michael Graves, **Arata Isozaki**, and **Shiro Kuramata**.

Both groups produced pieces that were part functional and part artwork and which combined expensive and inexpensive materials as well as motifs from different historical periods and cultures. The result challenged traditional expectations of design: rather than celebrating the integrity of wood grain, wooden carcasses were covered with colored laminates—often employing more than one pattern on the same item.

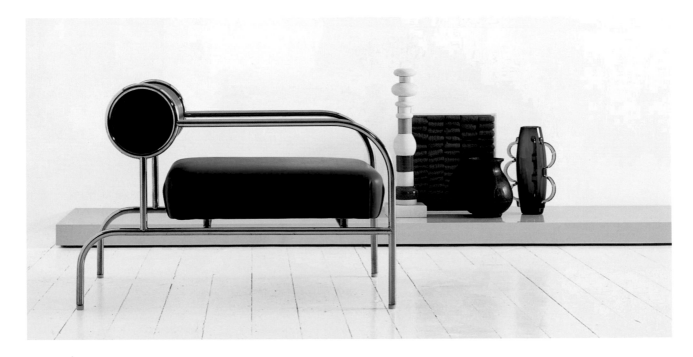

Much of **Gaetano Pesce**'s work is based on experiments with materials. His Nobody's chair was designed for fashion house Etro and incorporates fragments of the company's silk fabrics within panels of colored polyurethane-based elastic resin. 2004 35in (88cm) high ★ ★ ☆ ☆ ☆ ☆

The abandonment of form and function was not the only way in which designers around the world reacted to the new trend. Some reacted to Modernist symmetry by using asymmetrical shapes, structures, colors, and materials. In the U.S., Robert Venturi used bent wood laminates to create simplified versions of historical chairs—particularly Queen Anne and Art Deco styles. Both he and fellow American architect Michael Graves also brought traditional architectural forms into product design.

Within a decade an international economic improvement had ended with the 1987 crash, and the environment became an important factor. For many, recycling was the order of the day. The 1981 designs of the London-based Israeli designer **Ron Arad**, which included chairs made from car seats and corrugated cardboard, gained a new relevance. At the same time architect **Frank Gehry** created Experimental Edges, a collection of corrugated-cardboard furniture intended as art rather than design. These repeated the success of his 1970s Easy Edges cardboard furnishings, created in response to environmental issues.

At the same time Minimalism grew in popularity as a reaction to the excesses of Post Modernism. Like the Modernists, these designers aimed to be true to the materials they used, and they achieved this by employing clear glass and acrylic, metal and untreated wood.

Meanwhile, advances in technology allowed designers such as **Gaetano Pesce** to create sleek, injection-molded furniture or use computer-aided design to create designs without the need for prototypes. Accuracy and consistency could be guaranteed thanks to laser cutting. These hi-tech pieces contrasted with a return to handcrafts that saw those who had made their fortunes on the international money markets pay for expensive, one-off, handmade pieces. At the other end of the spectrum, thanks to internet communication, hand- and machine-manufacturing can be outsourced to low-wage countries.

By the turn of the 21st century, the cult of the designer had arrived and expensive, unique pieces became a means for the affluent to display their wealth. (This continued until the economic crash of 2008, when such displays became unappealing.) This freed designers to work in many disciplines and create pieces for clients with a global spread. People such as **Philippe Starck**, **Tom Dixon**, and **Marc Newson** created furniture, interiors, and products for manufacturers around the world and became household names thanks to promotion by companies including Alessi and Cappellini.

Other designers returned to their roots to make pieces that celebrated natural materials. Furniture by **Julia Krantz** and **Hugo França** in Brazil, ceramics by Americans **Peter Voulkos** and **Paul Chaleff**, and glass by American **Dale Chihuly** use traditional techniques to create modern works. There was also room for political pieces such as the **Campana Brothers**' Favela chair.

"Design" is now something for everyone: from kettles to pens, cars to sofas, we can all enjoy it.

Forrest Myers uses twisted aluminum coil to create loose yet rigid structures. His chairs are sculptures you can sit on—here pink and orange cube stools are set against a backdrop of his complex wire wall-hangings (*opposite*).

POST MODERN

The exuberance of Post Modernism places it directly opposite Modernism in the spectrum of 20th-century design movements. Its roots are in late 1970s and early 1980s Italy, where Studio Alchimia and the Memphis group of designers used modern and historic embellishments to decorate furniture, furnishings, and architecture. Ettore Sottsass, the leader of the Memphis group, explained it as follows: "It is important to realize that whatever we do or design has iconographic references, it comes from somewhere; any form is always metaphorical, never totally metaphysical; it is never a 'destiny' but always a fact with some kind of historical reference."

opposite, clockwise from top left Architectural paper lamps by **Isamu Noguchi** made from traditional Japanese mulberry-bark paper explore the concept of light as sculpture. Here they fill a corner of a Brooklyn town house to bring light and a timeless atmosphere to the family room. / The base of Isamu Noguchi's coffee table comprises two identical curved wood pieces that can be viewed from the sides or through the heavy plate-glass top. Placed on a deep shag-pile rug, it makes a sculptural statement. / The back of **Gaetano Pesce**'s Feltri armchair can be bent and positioned to suit the sitter, even forming its own arms. The frame is made from thick, resin-infused felt tied with string laces, while the seat is cushioned with padded, quilted fabric. / The sculptural Hand chair is **Pedro Friedeberg**'s most famous design and is typically surreal—the user sits on the palm and uses its fingers as an arm- and backrest. These chairs often feature a three-footed base and gilded finish.

right Amorphous shapes and contrasting colors combine in this **Karim Rashid** living room. The metal legs of the coffee table are the only shapes not to feature rounded edges or shades of pink and orange.

Designers revolt

Polychrome and printed laminates cover different sections of **Ettore Sottsass**'s Carlton shelf unit. The piece has become an icon of Memphis and Post Modern design. 1981 75in (190.5cm) wide ★ ★ ☆ ☆ ☆ ☆

Robert Venturi used molded plywood with an ebonized finish for the Sheraton chair he designed for Knoll. The playful design recalls 19th-century chairs, but its cut-out back features silkscreen-printed decoration and it has a black leather-upholstered seat pad. 1984 33.25in (84.5cm) high ★ ★ ★ ★ ★ ★

By the mid-1980s many designers had lost faith in Modernism and turned to the past for inspiration. This movement, known as Post Modernism, had been evolving since the mid-1960s. In 1966, in his paper "Complexity and Contradiction in Architecture," the American architect **Robert Venturi** rebelled against the purity of Modernism: "Architects can no longer afford to be intimidated by the puritanically moral language of orthodox Modern architecture. I like elements which are hybrid rather than 'pure,' compromising rather than 'clean,' distorted rather than 'straightforward,' ambiguous rather than 'articulated,' perverse as well as impersonal, boring as well as 'interesting,' conventional rather than 'designed,' accommodating rather than excluding, redundant rather than simple, vestigial as well as innovating, inconsistent and equivocal rather than direct and clear. I am for messy vitality over obvious unity. I include the non sequitur and proclaim the duality."

The key players in this new movement were a group of designers led by the architect **Ettore Sottsass** who called themselves the Memphis Group. The first exhibition of their New International Style was during the 1981 Salone del Mobile in Milan. Sottsass described it as, "Memphis tries to separate the object from the idea of functionalism. It is an ironic approach to the Modern notion of philosophical pureness. In other words, a table may need four legs to function but no one can tell me that the four legs have to look the same."

The result was colorful, characterful, and exciting furniture that had links to ancient and primitive cultures. Pieces such as Sottsass's Carlton bookcase, complete with Aztec-inspired elements, were decorated with plastic laminates in many colors rather than one type of wood veneer.

The members of Memphis came from a number of countries including: Italy (Sottsass and **Michele De Lucchi**), America (**Michael Graves**), the United Kingdom (**George J. Sowden**), France (**Martine Bedin**), Austria (**Hans Hollein**), Japan (**Arata Isozaki** and **Shiro Kuramata**), and Spain (**Javier Mariscal**).

The group's sense of fun can be seen in Mariscal's reimagined classic black leather and metal-framed chair. The Akaba S.A. Garriri chair was given a Mickey Mouse ears-shaped headrest and featured the cartoon character's unmistakable shoes at the ends of its legs.

Michael Graves was acclaimed for his Post Modern architecture, such as the Portland Public Services Building in Portland, Oregon. For Memphis he created pieces that combined the highbrow with popular culture, such as rare wood veneers with cheap plastic laminates.

When Memphis disbanded in 1988 its co-founder Michele De Lucchi adopted a more rational and modest design style and focused on industrial design and architecture.

The New York company Swid Powell was founded in 1983 by **Nan Swid** and **Addie Powell**. It produced Post Modern tableware designed by many Memphis designers, including Graves, Sottsass, and Venturi. Swid explained: "I knew that very few people would ever live in houses designed by **Richard Meier** or Robert Venturi, but I thought they would like to experience that aesthetic level." The result was Post Modern design for

Geometry inspired the Kristall table by
Michele De Lucchi, designed for Memphis
Milan in 1981 (*above left*). It is made
from patterned, laminated wood and
plastic-covered steel. 19.5in (50cm) high
★★ ★ ★ ★ ★ new

Michele De Luchi's First chair (*above right*)
is a restrained combination of a plastic-
coated tubular-metal hoop back and legs
and laminated wooden disc seat, back, and
armrests. It was designed for Memphis in
1983. 33in (84cm) high ★ ★ ★ ★ ★ ★

The Hotel 21 Grande Suite armchair
designed by **Javier Mariscal** for Moroso in
1995 is proof that chairs do not have to be
symmetrical to be comfortable (*right*).
Metal legs support deep foam cushions
upholstered with multi-colored leather. 31.5in
(80cm) high NPA

Op Art designs decorate the seat of **Pedro Friedeberg**'s Butterfly chair. A human head and feet add to the surreal effect (*above*). 13.5in (35cm) high ★ ★ ☆ ☆ ☆

In this open-plan living/dining area, Oh dining chairs by **Karim Rashid** surround the long dining table designed by **Peter Franck** and **Kathleen Triem** (*opposite*).

the mass market. Notable pieces include Graves's Little Dripper tea service, which has elements of Art Deco design, and Venturi's Grandmother pattern dinner service, an ironic, stylized reimagining of a chintz tablecloth, updated with black lines. It embodied Venturi's conviction that although the style of our immediate past, such as that of our parents, seems in bad taste, the buffer of a generation can make our grandparents' style appealing.

One key designer who was not a member of Memphis was **Alessandro Mendini**, a partner in Milan's Studio Alchimia and who favored an academic approach in contrast to Sottsass's instinctive one. The studio began in 1976, and Sottsass and De Lucchi were among the collaborators. It aimed to produce highly desirable products from affordable, kitsch materials that rejected Modernism. Its early exhibitions—Bau. Haus 1 and Bau. Haus 2—parodied Bauhaus furniture by replacing the clean lines of the originals with dramatic colors, mismatched legs, and sloping surfaces.

Pieces such as the lacquered wood, aluminum, and glass Mikiolone shelving unit designed by Mendini in collaboration with **Alessandro Guerriero** in 1986, which combined a wooden carcass with enameled wooden legs, brightly colored laminate surfaces, and glass shelves, paved the way for Memphis.

During the mid-1980s and early 1990s American **Wendell Castle** stopped making the organic, sculptural furniture from stacked, laminated wood for which he had become known. Instead, he looked to form, color, and concept to define his work, making furniture that had little to do with function.

Italian designer **Gaetano Pesce** was involved in many of the "avant-garde" movements of the 20th century. In the 1980s he moved to New York and began to make colorful, idiosyncratic furniture from resin, which he described as "poorly made" but which received critical acclaim.

The final years of the 20th century also saw designers bringing an ecological sensitivity to their work. In 1972 American architect **Frank Gehry** created a collection of affordable furniture made from cardboard reinforced with laminates and metal rods, called Easy Edges. He followed it a decade later with a collection of cardboard art furniture called Experimental Edges. Gehry went one step further in 1990–92 with a series of chairs for Knoll constructed from woven plywood.

Italian-born **Pedro Friedeberg** lives and works in Mexico City creating surreal artworks that include wood clocks with hands showing 1 to 12 fingers for numerals and legs and feet for a base, and chairs shaped like a carved hand.

The work of the designer **Karim Rashid**, who was born in Egypt but is now a U.S. citizen, is often described as "sensual" Minimalism, featuring soft shapes and bright colors. He has created more than 3,000 designs, including the Oh chair for Umbra, manhole covers for the sewers of New York, perfume bottles for Kenzo, the Bobble water bottle, and watches and tableware for Alessi.

The decorative appeal of **Alessandro Mendini** and **Alessandro Guerriero**'s Mikiolone— Nr. 2980 cocktail cabinet is more important than its function. Designed for Studio Alchimia, the turquoise laminated-wood carcass is decorated with yellow and blue enamel and has silver-gray enameled wooden legs. The glass shelves protrude from the sides. 1986 65in (162cm) high ★ ★ ☆ ☆ ☆

Ettore Sottsass

The Austrian-born Italian architect and designer **Ettore Sottsass** (1917–2007) is probably best known today as the founder of the Memphis design group, which did much to influence design and the Post Modern movement during the 1980s. However, he created many notable designs from the 1950s until his death.

Sottsass established his own architecture office in Milan in 1947 and, following a month working for the celebrated American designer **George Nelson** in New York, began working for the office equipment company Olivetti, which at the time was at the forefront of a technological revolution. He was appointed artistic director of the design company Poltronova in 1957.

During the late 1960s Sottsass started to turn away from the constraints of the Modern movement, and by the late 1970s he had become one of the most influential members of the Post Modern movement. "When I was young, all we ever heard about was functionalism, functionalism, functionalism," he is reported to have said. "It's not enough. Design should also be sensual and exciting." Sottsass's work at the time, like that of his colleagues, was brash and colorful. He used a wide range of materials and took a playful approach to form and function.

In 1981 he founded the Memphis group (named after a Bob Dylan song), a collective of international architects and designers based in Milan. It survived for eight years. Memphis took the experimental theme, unconventional materials, historic forms, kitsch motifs, and gaudy colors first used by Studio Alchimia. Their furniture—often made by traditional craftsmen—was decorated with colored plastic laminates emblazoned with kitsch geometric and leopard-skin patterns or made from printed glass, celluloid, neon tubes and zinc-plated sheet metal. For example, the Beverly cabinet Sottsass made in Memphis's first year featured green and yellow "snakeskin" laminate doors with brown "tortoiseshell" bookshelves set at an angle and a bright red light bulb.

The group's members produced furniture, lighting, ceramics, clothing, and jewelry in what they described as the "New International Style." Their pieces were exhibited all over the world. Sottsass left in early 1985.

He went on to concentrate on Sottsass Associati, an architecture and design group where he worked with former Memphis members and younger collaborators. His designs included a chain of shops for Esprit and a series of private houses (including one in Palo Alto for industrial designer David Kelley) as well as public buildings, notably Malpensa 2000 airport near Milan. Sottsass also continued to design glass and ceramics. He was one of the most important grandees of late 20th-century design.

The entrance to a doorway is framed by a monumental ceramic totem by **Ettore Sottsass**.

The Solo glass fruit bowl is **Ettore Sottsass**'s Post Modern reworking of the traditional tazza form popular with Murano factories. It was designed for Memphis in 1982. 10.5in (26cm) high ★★ ☆ ☆ ☆ ☆

The red and white plastic Sinus desk or table lamp designed for Stilnovo can be used vertically or horizontally. 1970 12.75in (32.4cm) high ★★ ☆ ☆ ☆ ☆

Made at Bitossi for the Memphis group, the sections of this totem can be rearranged. It is hand-signed "PA/E8 Ettore Sottsass Primo." 67.5in (171.5cm) high ★★ ☆ ☆ ☆ ☆

The two-tiered body of the Clesitera vase is multi-colored glass with suspended shapes. It is marked "E. Sottsass for Memphis by Toso Vetri d'Arte." 1986 19.5in (49.5cm) high ★★ ☆ ☆ ☆ ☆

Knoll commissioned the Eastside armchair in 1982. The enameled tubular-steel legs have clear plastic feet, while the wooden frame is upholstered and the back topped with a bolster. 32.5in (84cm) high ★ ☆ ☆ ☆ ☆ ☆

A range of pieces for Milan's Design Gallery form part of the Rovine/Ruins collection. This Compagnia Veteria Muranese limited-edition Le Connessoni Con LL Resto glass vase is number 3 from an edition of 9. 1992 18.5in (47cm) high NPA

Influential pieces

Expect the unexpected with Post Modern pieces. For some designers, the key was to take traditional ideas and turn them on their heads. So, **Robert Venturi**'s Grandmother pattern mug for Swid Powell reworked the chintz fabric he remembered from his grandmother's house and used it to decorate a dinner service. **Michael Graves** turned an Art Deco skyscraper into a bird's-eye maple dressing table decorated with colorful enamel panels. Maitland-Smith took a similar form and decorated it with a lacquered faux-wood-grain finish. Designers such as **Javier Mariscal** reduced furniture to an outline form created from wire, while **Wendell Castle** and **Karim Rashid** sculpt organic forms using metal or plastic as a base. **Frank Gehry** showed the sculptural possibilities of corrugated cardboard with his Easy Edges series.

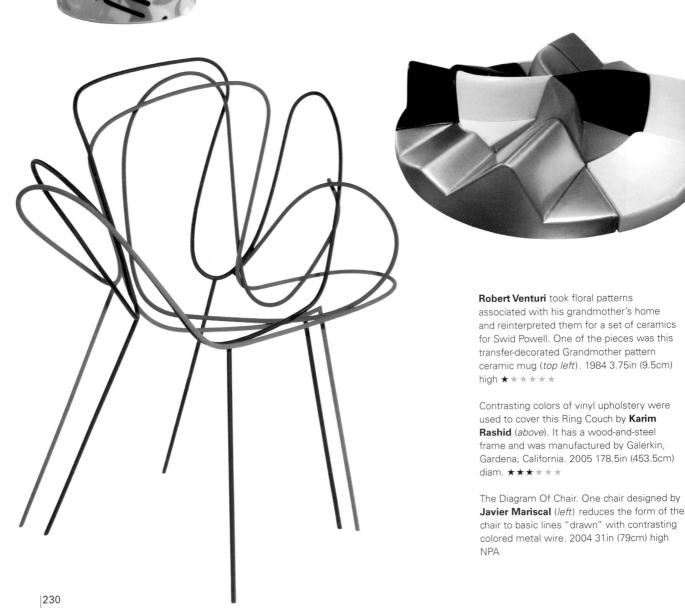

Robert Venturi took floral patterns associated with his grandmother's home and reinterpreted them for a set of ceramics for Swid Powell. One of the pieces was this transfer-decorated Grandmother pattern ceramic mug (*top left*). 1984 3.75in (9.5cm) high ★ ★ ★ ★ ★ ★

Contrasting colors of vinyl upholstery were used to cover this Ring Couch by **Karim Rashid** (*above*). It has a wood-and-steel frame and was manufactured by Galerkin, Gardena, California. 2005 178.5in (453.5cm) diam. ★ ★ ★ ★ ★ ★

The Diagram Of Chair. One chair designed by **Javier Mariscal** (*left*) reduces the form of the chair to basic lines "drawn" with contrasting colored metal wire. 2004 31in (79cm) high NPA

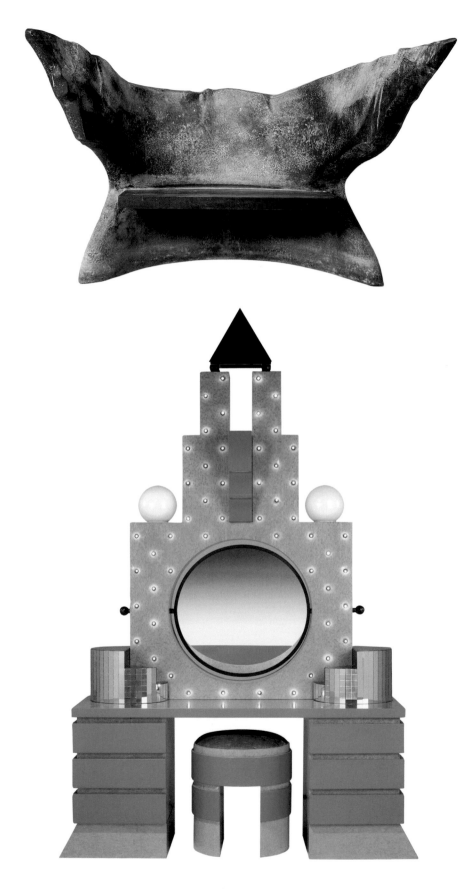

A lacquered faux-wood finish contrasts with the architectural form of this "skyscraper" cabinet by Maitland-Smith (*above*). It is fitted with 21 drawers, 2 cupboards and a pullout slide. 1970s 18.75in (47.5cm) wide ★★ ★ ★ ★ ★

The sculptural, organic Angel chair series is considered to be **Wendell Castle**'s finest achievement. This is a rare faceted painted bronze example (*above right*). c.1990 63in (175cm) wide ★★★★ ★ ★

Skyscrapers inspired **Michael Graves**'s architectural Plaza dressing table and matching upholstered stool designed for Memphis (*right*). It is made from maple root with an enameled teal finish, and incorporates a pivoting mirror flanked by stepped, mirrored pedestals and illuminated by small low-voltage light bulbs. 1981 Dressing table 55.5in (141cm) wide ★★★ ★ ★ ★

Frank Gehry's Wiggle chair from the Easy Edges series of practical, laminated cardboard furniture, which was designed to be affordable and meet the need for designers to be aware of environmental concerns (*left*). 1972 22in (56cm) high ★ ★ ☆ ☆ ☆ ☆

The Little Beaver armchair and ottoman are part of **Frank Gehry**'s Experimental Edges series and were made by Vitra (*below*). These generously proportioned pieces have a rough, ragged surface. They were made from strips of thick, corrugated cardboard and are both sculpture and surprisingly comfortable furniture. Marked with brass tag, numbered 54/100. 1987 Chair 33.5in (85cm) wide ★ ★ ☆ ☆ ☆ ☆

In a corner of a master bedroom the attractive, flowing shape of **Frank Gehry**'s Wiggle chair contrasts with the rectilinear forms of an abstract painting by Figueras and a **Mies van der Rohe** Barcelona chair (*opposite*).

Alessandro Mendini

Poltrona di Proust 1978

As a partner in the Studio Alchimia design group, **Alessandro Mendini** (b.1931) was instrumental in the development of Post Modern style and was a forerunner of the Memphis group. Mendini trained as an architect, but has turned his hand to many skills; he also works as a designer, artist, theorist, and poet.

Alchimia was founded in Milan in 1976, and its members delighted in using clashing colors and patterns and awkward forms; they also successfully combined expensive and inexpensive materials. Mendini described its work as "a confusion of craft and industry" and as a retaliation against the practical elegance of Modern design. Mendini believes that ornamentation should be the starting point for design and that people no longer want to buy sterile, mass-produced items, but pieces with personality and soul. "Every person is different," he says, "so why shouldn't an object also be different?"

The Proust chair is his most famous design. With it, in 1978, Mendini began a furniture series of so-called redesigns in which he reinterpreted the shape and ornamentation of existing designs that were typical of their day. Two years previously, he had begun work on a fabric pattern for Cassina that was to be a reflection on the French writer Marcel Proust. While researching the upper-middle-class environment associated with Proust, Mendini came across a copy of a chair in the Neo-Baroque style of 18th-century France. He covered the chair completely with a fabric of a colorful, hand-painted swarm of dots. He also painted all parts of the chair, irrespective of their structure and purpose. Mendini succeeded in referencing Impressionism but also the Baroque.

Mendini aimed to use both "low" (such as painted metal and plastic) and "high" (such as crystal glass and polished wood) materials to create a look that was "full and violent." In his journalism, Mendini described this as "Banal Design"—a reference to the phrase "Bel Design" used after World War II to describe tasteful and practical furnishings. Banal Design reflected the complexity and confusion of late 20th-century life.

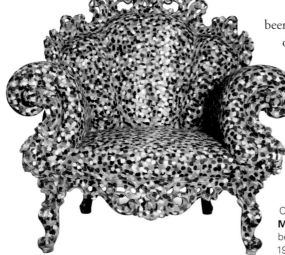

Mendini also claims that everything has already been invented and used; as a result he has concentrated on redesigning existing pieces and exhibits a great appreciation of decoration. For example, in the 1970s he redesigned **Gerrit Rietveld**'s Zig-Zag chair with a cruciform back, reworked **Gio Ponti**'s Superlegera chair by adding colored pennants to the legs and stiles, and added superficial ornament to **Marcel Breuer**'s Wassily chair.

Created as a "redesign" of a Louis XV chair, **Alessandro Mendini**'s Proust chair is an exaggerated version of a Rococo bergère decorated with a multi-colored, pointillist-inspired design. 1978 36.5in (93cm) wide ★★☆☆☆

The Geometrica version of the Proust chair is upholstered with a bold geometric fabric.
A **Ronan** and **Erwan Bouroullec** Cloud bookcase provides the backdrop.

Understated living

The belief that Post Modern interiors must be a zany cacophony of colors, shapes, and ideas is not always borne out. Often, all it takes is one or two well-chosen pieces to show how a room can be enhanced by the addition of something totally unexpected in an otherwise normal setting. However, rooms can be decorated in true Post Modern style, combining distorted pieces and bright hues for an exciting effect.

Many Post Modern rooms feature walls and floors decorated with cool, neutral coverings that provide a backdrop for the movement's boldly colored furnishings and ornaments—perhaps just one bold piece or a collection of objects—which then become the focus of the room.

Where color is used on every surface, it is often concentrated in large blocks of contrasting colors rather than a chorus of different shades. For example, the designer **Karim Rashid** uses blocks of pink offset by white and yellow to create a cohesive color scheme that complements many of his own furniture and accessory designs.

The result should be a space that combines comfort with an unconventional mixture of materials and angles.

In this living room, a pair of sofas by **Christian Liaigre** serves to balance the graphic quality of the wall-hung sculpture that dominates the room. The pair of benches at the end of the coffee table are by **Bruno Romeda**. The calm beige and black color scheme proves that Post Modern interiors do not have to be a riot of color.

Combining Modernist and Post Modern furnishings creates a welcoming corner in a small hallway (*left*). **Isamu Noguchi**'s Akari lamp provides diffused light for anyone using the vintage **Mies van der Rohe** daybed, and illuminates a Tauba Auerbach drawing.

A glass-topped table provides a simple setting for a collection of black-and-white ceramics by **Ettore Sottsass** (*below*).

Shades of pink contrast with white in this room designed by **Karim Rashid** (*left*). The amorphous shapes contrast with the metal base of the coffee tables and the rings of the appliqué wall light.

Karim Rashid's design encompasses all elements of the home (*above*). This room features one of his wallpaper designs and a DJ mixing-desk pod he created for the Canadian company Pure Design.

Blocks of bold color mark out the different uses of a white box loft space (*opposite*). The rectangular area—highlighted by the colored recess above—houses the bathroom and utility areas. Behind the yellow Plexiglas panel is the main bathroom. The ceiling shows the position of the kitchen and dining area.

MINIMALIST

Crisp, clean-cut, and spare, Minimalism provides clean, light spaces for living. As they are free of clutter, the furnishings are able to take center stage. The style was a reaction to the excesses of Post Modernism, and designers returned to the simple, functional shapes that defined the Modern era—only this time shapes were spare and lacked any ornamentation at all. Rooms were stripped back to the bare essentials and featured textures and unusual furnishings by famous-name designers such as **Tom Dixon** and **Philippe Starck** to create focal points rather than paintings or sculpture. The result is calming, elegant, and often eclectic.

opposite, clockwise from top left **Tom Dixon**'s Jack is more than just a light—you can sit on it and stack it, too. The plastic, graphic form uses the process of rotary molding. It was launched in 1994 to prove that industrial manufacturing was still possible in the U.K. / The body of **Marc Newson**'s Felt chair is created from sculpted, reinforced fiberglass designed to look like folded felt fabric. The supporting leg is made from natural polished aluminum. / A high-tech base contrasts with a simple glass top on this **Norman Foster** table. As with Foster's buildings, furnishings like these are designed to maximize the sense of space in a room. / Dense swirls of twisted wire with a pink anodized finish create one of **Forrest Myers**'s signature chairs.

right An abstract painting enhances the simplicity of this hallway designed by architect **John Pawson**. A small wooden stool with a leather seat is the only furniture.

Proving that a chair does not need four legs, **Philippe Starck**'s sleek and ergonomic Ed Archer chair is made from stitched and laced saddle leather upholstery, over a tubular-steel frame with aluminum rear leg. 1986 38.5in (98cm) high ★★ ☆ ☆ ☆ ☆

An update on the Modernist cantilevered chair, **Shiro Kuramata**'s Sing, Sing, Sing armchair has a coated-steel seat and backrest designed to have a slight spring to add to its comfort. The chair was manufactured by XO. 1985 33.5in (85cm) high ★★ ☆ ☆ ☆ ☆

Cleaning house

In the 1970s some designers in the U.S. returned to the strict, minimalist principles of the early Modernist movement. This was partly prompted by cost-cutting by manufacturers and partly by a desire to reverse the trend for disposable furnishings, which scientists were already warning would bring about the destruction of the planet.

By the late 1980s this had developed into a simpler, clean style described as "New Minimalism," "Late Modern," or even "Dematerialization." Furniture was made without applied decoration, from clear acrylic or wicker, among other materials. These pieces started to become witty in the 1990s, using found objects, or had the smooth lines of designs created on a computer.

Japanese designer **Shiro Kuramata** combined eastern minimalism and western whimsy to create original and imaginative furniture. His minimalist How High the Moon chair and sofa reconsiders the form of the classic armchair. There is no visible support or interior frame and so the sitter appears to float on it. Other designs use translucent acrylic, glass and aluminum.

Like Kuramata, designers such as **Philippe Starck** and **Marc Newson** went in their own design directions rather than following a particular trend to create pieces with great visual impact.

Starck, a French designer and architect, made his name designing the Café Costes near the Pompidou Center in Paris. This led to the first of many architectural and interior commissions, and international fame. From the late 1980s onwards, he turned his skills to designing an extensive range of household objects, from chairs to door handles, lemon squeezers to lighting. Many of his designs are based on classic forms, reduced to the bare essentials and then given a Post Modern twist such as using a hat as a lampshade or making chair legs from different materials. Early pieces by Starck used wood and metal, but by the 1990s most of his work was plastic, resulting in greater flexibility in his designs and more affordable pieces.

Marc Newson is among the most prolific and internationally renowned designers Australia has produced. His work is inspired by futuristic Italian furniture from the 1960s and '70s by designers such as **Joe Colombo**. His sculptural Lockheed Lounge (1985) was made from fiberglass and riveted aluminum and was similar in form to the 1950s aircraft from which it took its name. As well as garnering critical acclaim, it resulted in the chance to work with a new Japanese company, Idée. Newson worked there from 1987 until 1991, creating unusual furniture that updated popular forms from the 1950s. In the 1990s he moved to Europe, but his work continued to reference his native Australia, with bold shapes reminiscent of surfboards and bright colors that suggest sun and sand.

Tom Dixon began making furniture in the 1980s from salvaged materials, such as scrap metal, reclaimed kitchen utensils, and rubber tubing. This self-taught designer says he designs "mainly through an interest in materials and technologies." His first commercial success came in 1989 with the S-chair, an homage to **Verner Panton**'s chair of the same name made from a metal frame covered with woven marsh straw. Within a decade Dixon was known around the

The slim, sculptural, organic form of **Tom Dixon**'s S-chair—created by weaving marsh straw on a metal frame—provides a focal point in this cool and tranquil bathroom. A pair of mirrors appears to stretch to infinity above the washbasin.

A rustic wooden table contrasts with a set of Ghost chairs by **Philippe Starck**. These witty injection-molded polycarbonate chairs pare back the shape of a classic Louis XVI armchair to lines and shadows.

world for his innovative pieces, such as the Bird rocking chair, which consisted of a simple tick-shaped wooden frame covered with foam and fabric. He went on to be design director of Habitat, bringing the work of designers including Verner Panton, **Ettore Sottsass**, and Newson to mass-market consumers.

In contrast to Dixon's work, furniture made by Brazil-based **Julia Krantz** shows her interest in ecology and nature. She carves her sculptural designs from stack-laminated plywood; the result is smooth, glossy, organic shapes. The flowing lines of the plywood layers and carved surface often suggest water or the folds in a piece of fabric. She set up her company, Julia Krantz Movelaria, in 2000.

Perhaps the most enduring household name of the 20th century is Alessi. The Italian homewares company was established in 1921 as a foundry and metal workshop. But in the 1950s it started to commission celebrated designers to create homewares. The range took off in the 1970s when innovative designers such as **Alessandro Mendini** and Ettore Sottsass started to create unconventional furniture, ceramics, and glassware for it. The true turning point came in 1983 when Mendini invited 11 international architects, including **Michael Graves**, **Richard Meier** and **Aldo Rossi**, to design tea and coffee sets for the firm. The Tea and Coffee Piazza brought international acclaim and set the pattern for the company's reputation for high-quality pieces with an avant-garde edge. Among its most successful pieces are Graves's Whistling Bird kettle, Philippe Starck's Juicy Salif lemon squeezer, and Mendini's Anna G corkscrew.

Graves trained as an architect and went on to work for George Nelson, where he discovered the possibilities of modern product design. His success as an architect led to his being commissioned by the Memphis group and Alessi. His work is influenced by historical styles: for Memphis he created the Piazza dressing table, based on an Art Deco skyscraper, and for Alessi the Mantel clock, which is based on Classical architecture.

By the later 20th century, technological developments meant that strong, thin wire could be used to create textured, abstract chairs that appear to be sculpture rather than furniture. **Javier Mariscal** used wire to do little more than create an outline for his Diagram of a Chair. One. In contrast to this, **Forrest Myers** used a jumble of tubular black metal for the seat of his armchairs and a metal grid over springs and rolled armrests for a sofa. **John Risley** took a figurative approach for a lounge chair and ottoman. **André Dubreuil**'s Trône iron chair is an exaggerated wrought-iron wing chair with an upholstered seat.

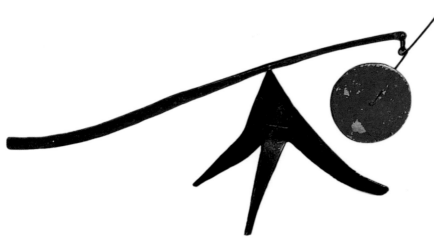

The Super Guppy floor lamp **Marc Newson** designed for Idee shows his confidence in using linear forms (*above*). The lamp is made from aluminum and set on casters to make it easy to move around the room. 1987 73in (185.5cm) high ★ ★ ☆ ☆ ☆ ☆

Alexander Calder was a pioneer of the mobile—a kinetic sculpture made with delicately balanced or suspended components that move in response to air currents (*left*). c.1960 8in (20cm) wide ★ ★ ★ ★ ☆ ☆

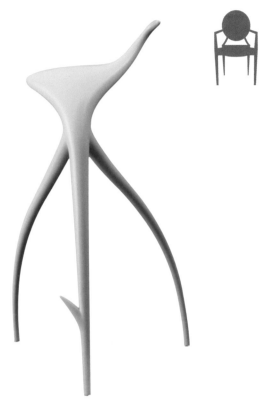

Influential pieces

Advances in technology allowed designers to create chairs that appear to be more sculpture than seat. Despite its appearance, **Philippe Starck**'s W-W stool is a comfortable bar stool with a rest for one foot. **André Dubreuil**'s Trône and **Tom Dixon**'s Pylon chair used strong, thin wire to create textured and abstract chairs that are little more than a frame. **Marcel Wanders** used carbon fiber to create a Knotted chair that appeared to be made of knotted string. More ergonomic chairs were designed by **Arata Isozaki**, who used the actress Marilyn Monroe's curves to shape the backrest of his birchwood Monroe chair. Similar curves can be seen in **Marc Newson**'s Embryo chair; its waisted shape is covered with neoprene, a material usually used to make wetsuits.

Philippe Starck designed the sand-cast aluminum W-W stool for the film director Wim Wenders (*above left*). Such was the demand for this biomorphic stool, with its spur footrest that it is now produced by Vitra. 1990 38in (98.5cm) high ★★ ★ ★ ★ ★

A slubbed fabric seat contrasts with the wrought-iron frame of **André Dubreuil**'s Trône chair (*left*). The bent and welded shield back rises to an exaggerated scroll. c.1985 56.75in (144cm) high ★★★ ★ ★ ★

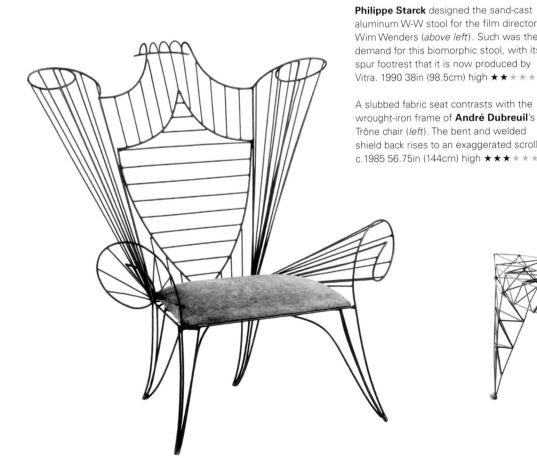

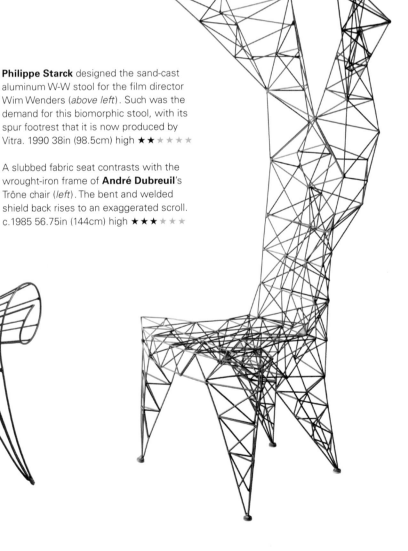

Industrial techniques combine with handcrafts in Marcel Wanders's lightweight Knotted chair (*left*). An aramid and carbon-fiber thread is knotted into shape, impregnated with epoxy resin and hung in a frame to dry, allowing gravity to shade the final form. The chair was a result of Droog's 1996 Dry Tech I project. 25in (64cm) wide ★★ ★ ★ ★ new

Arata Isozaki used Marilyn Monroe's figure as the inspiration for the back of his Monroe chair (*right*). 1973, re-issued by Tendo Mokko 2004 21in (54cm) wide ★★ ★ ★ ★

Tom Dixon says that designing his steel wire Pylon chair "felt like a crash course in structural engineering" (*left*). 1992 23.75in (60cm) wide ★★ ★ ★ ★ ★ new

The neoprene-covered, elegant, narrow-waisted Embryo chair by **Marc Newson** has a tubular-steel and aluminum frame (*right*). c.1988 30.5in (77.5cm) high ★★ ★ ★ ★

SHIRO KURAMATA

How High the Moon chair 1986

The Japanese designer **Shiro Kuramata** was born in Tokyo in 1934. Prior to opening his own design studio in the city in 1965, he had received training in traditional Japanese woodcraft at secondary school, worked as a cabinetmaker at the Teikoku Kizai furniture factory, studied western concepts of interior design at the Kuwasawa design school, and conceived displays and product for the small San-Ai and the giant Matsuya department stores. This grounding in the theoretical and in practical, and in both traditional oriental and modern western aesthetics, gave rise to an innovative and highly distinct style evident throughout Kuramata's impressive body of work—produced both prior to his joining the Memphis group at its founding in 1981 and thereafter until his death in 1991.

Underpinning Kuramata's designs is an extensive use of industrial, rather than organic, materials, such as acrylic, glass, aluminum, and steel mesh. However, inspired by Minimalist and Surrealist philosophies, it is the manner in which they are deployed that lies at the heart of his style. Above all there is a tremendous sense of lightness and transparency, and something of a floating sensation—as if his interiors and artifacts have been released from gravity. Much of this is achieved by the removal of what Kuramata called "visual impurities."

This striving for lightness and for clarity and purity of line is, however, most evident in Kuramata's now iconic furniture designs, and especially his 1986 How High the Moon armchairs and sofas, and his 1998 Miss Blanche armchair. The latter, named after the central character in Tennessee Williams's drama *A Streetcar Named Desire*, comprises Plexiglas red roses suspended in a clear acrylic resin frame. The effect is to make a hugely heavy 155-pound (70 kg) chair appear to weigh next to nothing. The ingenuity of this is even more pronounced in the How High the Moon pieces. Named after the 1940s jazz standard, and with a shimmering, moonlike, nickel-plated, and epoxy resin-coated finish, its steel mesh on a steel matrix frame is very heavy. However, also constructed with meticulous attention to detail (there are some 2,300 soldered joints in each one), the final form appears almost featherlike, and floating in a celestial realm—and that is not so much a deception as an ingenious sleight-of-hand, and one very characteristic of Kuramata.

The nickel-plated wire mesh of **Shiro Kuramata**'s How High the Moon chair means that it appears to float in the air. 1986 27.5in (70cm) wide ★★ ☆ ☆ ☆ ☆

The technical prowess of the How High the Moon chair is enhanced by a natural setting. Here, a plain white wall and wooden floor serve as a contrast to its wire form.

Clutter-free zones

Minimalist rooms provide a quiet retreat for busy people. Bare, white walls and a few simple pieces of furniture do not allow for clutter or collections—just a peaceful space where it may be possible to find a Zen-like calm.

Hallmarks of the style are plain walls, occasionally interrupted by a painting or two; tall, built-in cupboards to hide the necessities of life; doorways with no doors to allow the light into every corner; large windows with simple blinds to draw at night or create a diffused light; and plain floors occasionally softened by a large rug.

In these large, airy, stripped-down rooms, the furnishings either become part of the cool, white experience or are made the focal point. Wooden furniture based on vernacular designs provides a gentle contrast with the plain walls, while large white sofas and shelves blend into the background. However, bold or colorful, contemporary pieces can be used to add a splash of unexpected texture or color and prevent the overall effect from appearing sterile. By paring rooms down to their necessary elements, minimalist interiors offer a tranquil atmosphere that can provide an escape from the hubbub of daily life.

There is no denying that **John Pawson**'s interiors are minimalist. However, his use of warm white walls, natural wood surfaces and simple wooden furniture makes them welcoming rather than austere. Here, the dining room leads on to the kitchen at the back of the house with a wall of floor-to-ceiling cupboards opposite the fireplace (*below*). Hidden storage is the key to living in a minimalist environment. An open door in the wall of flush cupboards in the dining room (*opposite*) reveals shelves for storing bottles of wine and water.

A few well-chosen pieces are all you need for stylish, minimal living. This **John Pawson** living room is furnished with a J16 rocking chair and rattan folding chair by **Hans Wegner** (*above*). A sculpture by **Ken Price** sits on the stone bench.

In a large, industrial space, a white Lazy Working Sofa by **Philippe Starck** with integrated tables and lamps at each arm takes center stage beneath a window in the living room (*opposite*).

Only a very spacious room could accommodate this floor-to-ceiling fireplace. Here, a gigantic steel box appears to be a section of wall. It is a welcome feature in the white space, and although the fireplace is not huge, it supplements the room's under-floor heating.

Ingenuity is in demand when you need stylish yet practical storage. In this house by **Guy Peterson** in Sarasota, Florida (*top*), a plasma screen is mounted above a custom-built metal-clad unit that pulls out, opens up, and houses all the entertainment equipment. To add to the architectural feel, the top of the unit is fashioned from a concrete slab.

Simplicity is key to the effective design of this bedroom. A long sideboard provides essential storage, but also doubles as a place to display favorite objects. The pair of identical mirrors that hang above adds an illusion of space (*above*).

The free-flowing, organic form and bright blue of **Marc Newson**'s fiberglass Orgone chaise longue contrasts with the simple wooden furniture that surrounds it (*left*).

A single block of marble was the starting point for **Marc Newson**'s Low Voronoi shelf (*below*). It is carved with a series of rounded cells that bring an organic feel to one wall of an open-plan living area.

A pair of **Paul McCobb** chairs creates a cozy corner for reading or conversation. Part of the Planner Group he devised for the Winchendon Furniture Company, these chairs exhibit good proportion and line, combining beauty with honesty of function and form. Like other pieces in the range, they use traditional birch and maple and simple construction in an undecorated, modular fashion. They were among the best-selling contemporary furniture lines of the 1950s, and were in continuous production from 1949 until 1964.

REUSE

The need to protect the planet and the desire to express individuality encouraged designers to create pieces that reused or recycled materials or made a statement about society. The demand for "design" means that designers no longer have to restrict themselves to one discipline; instead, they can work in many fields. Thanks to companies such as Alessi, their work is mass-produced and promoted and sold to the large numbers of design-aware consumers, as well as to wealthy clients who can afford one-off or limited-edition pieces. The result is interiors filled with an eclectic mix of pieces that celebrate the many facets of 21st-century design.

opposite, clockwise from top left A slim, sculptured oak trunk provides a frame for a forged-steel base and branches for **Danny Lane**'s Viking table. The result is more sculpture than furniture. / A marriage of creativity and technology, **Ron Arad**'s Bookworm bookshelf can be manipulated into multiple shapes without compromising its strength or functionality. Initially designed as a one-off piece for the 1993 Milan Furniture Fair, it is now mass-produced in injection-molded PVC by Kartell and has become one of Arad's best-selling works. / The metal tube frame of the **Campana Brothers**' Cipria couch is hidden by nine pillows, each one a different shape and covered with ecological fur with different hair lengths. The result is whimsical and inviting.

right A **Curtis Jeré** starburst wall sculpture provides a focal point. The metal rods radiating from the center are echoed in the base of the fiberglass and maple **Eames** chair.

Fernando and **Humberto Campano** were inspired by the shanty towns of their native Rio de Janeiro to create the Favela chair. Like the houses there, it is constructed from recycled materials. 2002 29in (74cm) high

★★ ☆ ☆ ☆ ☆ new

Texture and form are factors in the work of **Peter Voulkos**. This hand-built two-handled vessel has horizontal ridges and a filled-in top-to-bottom tear. 1980s 14in (35cm) high

★★★ ☆ ☆ ☆

A new purpose

Against a backdrop of colorful, humorous Post Modern design, a group of designer–makers used a combination of recycling and a crafts revival to create new pieces with an anti-corporate, DIY spirit. Names such as **Ron Arad**, **Peter Voulkos**, and **Humberto** and **Fernando Campana** used their designs to promote social and environmental issues and to campaign against consumerism, as an antidote to mass-produced, throwaway pieces. This was design with a message that continues to hit home. It reused and reconstructed existing items to new designs, often rough and ready in appearance.

Israeli-born Ron Arad set up One-Off Limited in London in 1981 and started to make a series of unique, experimental pieces of furniture. His early successes included Rover chairs, which were made from salvaged car seats welded to a tubular-steel frame base. He went on to use raw, industrial materials such as steel and concrete that suggest urban decay. These pieces included Concrete Sound, a turntable encased in distressed concrete. By the 1990s he was concentrating on a new venture—Ron Arad Associates—which creates more commercial pieces such as his bent laminated-plywood Empty chair, designed in 1993. The Bookworm bookcase Arad designed for Kartell in the mid-1990s remains a best-seller.

Arad once explained: "I have no problem designing stuff for Vitra or Moroso that is made to be sold in shops, but I also like to do big projects or products that cause people in the Bolshevik art world to be uncomfortable. But that's a problem of their perception. I don't want to stop doing anything. I want to do it all as seriously as I can, whether it's industrial or a useless installation."

The salvage element of this reused and reconstructed furniture was used by American-born glass sculptor **Danny Lane**, who works in London and combines stainless-steel supports with 1in (2.5cm)-thick glass to create a range of chairs and tables. Americans **Jerry Fels** and **Curtis Freiler** took a similar approach to the pieces they created for Artisan House studio from the 1950s onwards, working as **Curtis Jeré.** For example, their Flashlight floor lamp/sculpture featured a torch-shaped head on a simple metal stand.

Greek-American ceramicist Peter Voulkos created monumental clay sculptures that showed that clay could produce more than tablewares and decorative figures. His work at the Otis College of Art and Design (formerly the Los Angeles County Art Institute) and later at the University of California at Berkeley was inspired by the work of the Abstract Expressionists, especially the painter Franz Kline, who believed that monumentalism would redeem decorative art. Like them, he worked in a seemingly spontaneous and intense way to create works with a dramatic impact.

Voulkos worked by creating freeform vessels, decorated with torn, ripped, and gouged surfaces, left plain or covered with painted brushstrokes or rich, colorful glazes. Later he stacked clay pots together to create a single object, using the ancient technique of building up ropes of clay to make vessels, and experimented with different clay bodies and the effects of wood smoke and charcoal in the kiln. He also set up a bronze foundry and used it to create monumental sculptures for public and private commissions.

Albert Paley began his career making bold jewelry designed to move with the human body. But he has gone on to create sculpture in a similar sensual, organic style that both enhances and is enhanced by its surroundings. He twists forged steel into sinuous, flowing shapes reminiscent of Art Nouveau and northern European metalwork.

Paley once explained: "Usually people think of metal in its industrial state—bars and rods and plates—but metal is very plastic. It can be formed and shaped into anything: cold, through hydraulic bending, or by heating it to a yellow state. People are amazed at how fluid the steel is in my work, how alive it seems. On one side these tendril ribbon shapes are woven through the structure to indicate water, and I had to make solid steel seem translucent."

Form, color, and texture inform of the work of Humberto and Fernando Campana. The work of these brothers is consistent with the rudimentary furniture beginning to emerge at the end of the 1980s. They use scrap wood and fabrics, plastic hosing and drain covers to create highly individual furniture that reflects the street culture of their native Brazil. The concept of a jumbled mass is frequently seen in their work. For example, the piece that brought them international renown—the Vermelha (red) chair—was made from red cord bought at a street market and wound around a metal frame.

This movement is, by its very nature, in a constant state of flux, development, and renewal.

The colors and textures of the different metals used add to the striking form of a **Curtis Jeré** wall sculpture (*above*). They complement the black and gold accessories on the shelf beneath them.

The twisted and molded steel base of this **Danny Lane** table are set off by the plate-glass top (*below*). The sculpted edge of the glass is designed to catch and reflect the light. Late 1980s–early '90s 66.5in (170cm) wide ★ ★ ★ ☆ ☆ ☆

Campana Brothers

The work of Brazilians **Humberto** and **Fernando Campana** has a low-tech, rough-and-ready finish that celebrates and commentates on their homeland. For example, the 2003 Multidao chair consists of dozens of handmade rag dolls on a chair frame and makes an unsettling comment on the huge populations found in Brazil's cities.

The brothers started working together in 1983 and gained international attention in 1989 with a furniture exhibition entitled Gli inconfortabili (The Inconsolable), which was more concerned with politics than functional objects. Their use of unremarkable and recycled materials—including industrial rubbish—to make handmade items encapsulates their belief in the potential for social redemption.

Despite the apparent rudimentary construction of their furniture—Humberto originally studied law and Fernando architecture—their work is bought by affluent U.S. and European customers. They also use waste materials in their furniture. Their Sushi range of furniture takes advantage of the different thicknesses of waste textiles including synthetics, wool, and boiled wool. The fabrics are rolled up together then sliced to create multi-colored concentric rings that are used to cover tabletops and upholster chairs. A variation on this technique creates a low, soft seat by stuffing rolled strips of fabric into a tubular frame. In 2013 the Campanas took the concept a step further, creating the "ocean" collection, wall and pendant mirrors framed with felt, rubber carpet and EVA in shades of green, blue, and white.

The haphazard appearance of the brothers' work is encapsulated in a series of pieces for the home, commissioned by Alessi in 2003. They made pieces including a fruit basket, candle holders, and a table made from stainless-steel rods. The rods are arranged so that they appear to be suspended in the air as if in a game of pick up sticks. Similarly, the Nuvem range is made from tangled aluminum wire. Nuvem means "cloud" in Portuguese, and the random patterns in the wire used to create these bowls and mats look like clouds of wire.

In contrast to the rough-and-ready feel of their early work, the brothers' 2015 Estrella collection combined craftsmanship and high-end technology to create environmentally sustainable chairs and tables inspired by the *bolacha do mar*, a close relative of the starfish. Using laser-cut and welded metal covered with colored epoxy resin, a stylized representation of the sea creature is repeated in different sizes to create chairs, tables and lamps. "As many of our concepts, our inspiration came from nature," Humberto explained. "We imagined a colony of sea stars all together."

Cotton rope was used to create the seat of the **Campana Brothers'** Vermelha chair. But the apparently random design was actually carefully constructed. The messiness contrasts with this simple setting of plain white walls and a floor-to-ceiling window.

The **Campana Brothers** combined modern and recycled traditional materials for their Detonado sofa. The arms, backrest, and seat of the metal frame are covered with a nylon-reinforced patchwork of scraps of caning that have been left over after a chair is repaired. Made in a limited edition of 8. 2013 88.5in (225cm) long NPA ★★ ★ ★

The Verde—a standard metal chair wrapped in colored cotton—is a humorous variation on the Modernist chair. 1993 19in (48cm) wide ★★ ★ ★ ★ ★

The Multidao chair was inspired by local handmade rag dolls and celebrates traditional crafts. 2003 25in (63.5cm) high ★★★ ★ ★ ★ original

Multi-colored boiled wool, rubber, and foam strips were used to make the Sushi chair. 2002 23.5in (60cm) high NPA

The Esperança glass lamp was part of a collaboration with Venini and includes figures based on Brazilian dolls. 2010 22in (55cm) diam. NPA

The patchwork covering of the **Campanas'** Leather Works chair is gradually built up using scraps of leather to create the irregular finish (*left*). The leather is printed with varying grain sizes to add to the haphazard effect. 2007 33.5in (85cm) wide NPA

It takes four people to knot a 328-foot (100 m) velvet tube filled with polyurethane chips and goose down to create the **Campana Brothers'** Boa sofa (*below*). Since it has no frame, it relies on its irregular form for support. 2002. 63in or 75in (160cm or 190cm) wide NPA

Hand-bent steel wire is the only material used to create the Corallo armchair (*opposite*). The manufacturer Edra smoothes the wire to remove any sharp edges and covers it with an epoxy paint finish. 2004 57in (144.5cm) wide NPA

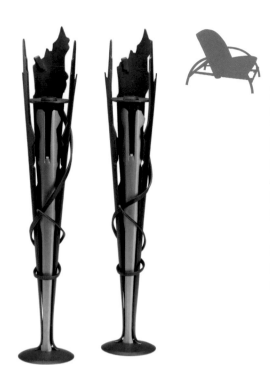

Influential pieces

Metal and glass enable designers to create sleek forms with shimmering or textured finishes from new and recycled materials. Traditionally used for outdoor furniture, these materials have found favor for interior pieces since **Ron Arad** used salvaged bent sheet steel, bolted into place, for his Well Tempered chair, while **Arman** was known for his furniture and sculptures inspired by found objects. The stacked, broken glass and rusting metal of **Danny Lane**'s furniture provides a contrast to the slick design world, particularly that of the 1980s. Sculptor **Albert Paley**, on the other hand, creates forged-steel, organic forms in which the metal appears to be almost fluid, in contradiction to the inflexible nature of the material.

Albert Paley's Vulcan candle holders consist of a fluid forged milled-steel frame with brass inserts (*above left*). 1994 20.25in (51.5cm) high
★★ ★ ★ ★ ★

Sheets of salvaged bent steel are bent and then bolted into place to create **Ron Arad**'s Well Tempered chair (*below*). The result is the outline—but not the bulk—of a traditional armchair. The chairs are made by Vitra. 1986 37.5in (94cm) wide ★★ ★ ★ ★ ★

Thanks to the four irregular stacked-glass supports, the top of **Danny Lane**'s Bird dining table appears to float above the stylized, mild-steel bird sculpture beneath it (*above*). 1998 89.5in (228cm) wide
★ ★ ★ ★ ★ ★

A sculptural base featuring a bronze cello and saxophone supports the glass top of this **Arman** dining table (*right*). Signed and numbered. 1987 44in (111.5cm) wide
★ ★ ★ ★ ★ ★

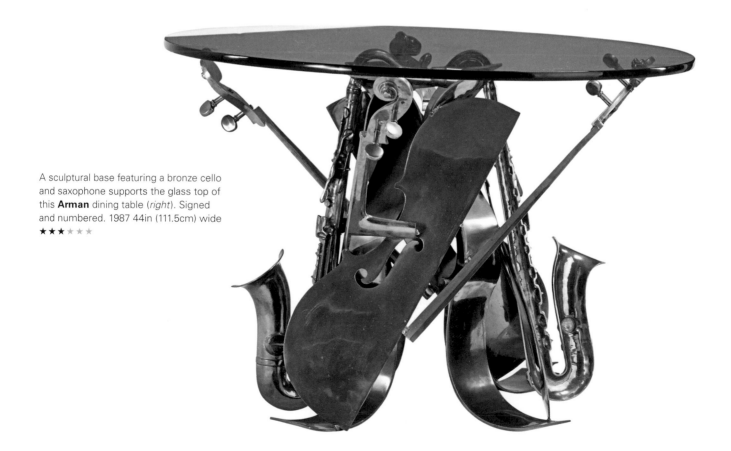

Ron Arad

Rover chair 1981

Born in Tel Aviv in 1951, Israeli architect and designer **Ron Arad** is a graduate of Jerusalem's Bezalel Academy of Arts and Design (1971–73) and the Architectural Association in London (1974–79). Since co-founding Arad Associates in 1989, he has produced a hugely impressive body of work. Architectural highlights include the Bauhaus Museum in Tel Aviv (2008) and the Design Museum in Holon (2010), which feature concrete and steel rendered in distinctive biomorphic shapes.

Steel, tempered and cut, and undoubtedly Arad's medium of choice, has also been employed in many of his product designs. His twisting and curvaceous, aptly named Bookworm bookcase, designed in 1993 and still produced by the Kartell company, is a stand-out example. Head of the Design Products Department at the Royal College of Art, London, from 1997 to 2009, Arad has also regularly embraced technological innovation—notably evident in the chandeliers he designed in 2005 for the Swarovski crystal company, which can receive and display through LEDs text messages from mobile phones.

However, it is not for the use of cutting-edge technology that Arad is best known. That honour falls to some chairs he designed at the outset of his career, prior to Arad Associates. Made from beaten, bent, welded, and polished steel, his now classic, cartoonlike takes on the plump, upholstered armchair—Well Tempered (1986) and Big Easy (1988)—are old-school blacksmith rather than hi-tech. Even more iconic, however, is the Rover chair he designed in 1981, and which initially featured a recycled, upholstered red leather front seat from a Rover 2000 motor car, which Arad had found in a scrapyard in north London. (When the chair went into production, more commonplace black rather than red seats were used.) Mounted on a tubular-steel scaffolding frame, this totally innovative composition was a fascinating fusion of contemporary thinking. The scaffold base was a wilfully rugged and affordable post-Punk take on the then fashionable High Tech style, exemplified by the Richard Rogers- and Renzo Piano-designed Pompidou Center in Paris, and Rogers's similarly "inside-out" Lloyd's building in London. The reused car seat is a thrifty make-do during the economic downturn of the period; and, with hindsight, prescient of recycling and the Green movement. Above all, however, Arad's Rover is an example of using what Marcel Duchamp, the founding father of conceptual art, called an *objet trouvé* (found object) and as such is ultimately admired not so much for the materials or the techniques, nor for the craftsmanship or ergonomics, but for the ingenuity of the idea.

The salvaged Rover car seat complete with its headrest and the industrial tubular-steel scaffolding frame encapsulates the spirit of the Reuse movement. 1981 38.5in (98cm) high ★★ ★ ★ ★ ★

In a large, urban living space the sturdy tubular frame and practical leather seat of the Rover complement concrete floors and distressed walls.

Salvage style

Furniture and accessories created by reusing materials create multifaceted rooms filled with color and texture. These statement pieces look particularly at home in spacious lofts and converted barns—you could almost call them recycled furnishings in recycled buildings. However, more intimate rooms also suit these pieces, perhaps putting them in a more intimate setting where their varied roots can still be appreciated.

Pieces made from salvaged materials work well in an interior when combined with furnishings made by craftsmen who aim to reinterpret traditional forms and techniques for modern living. Large-scale ceramic sculptures, experimental glass, and functional metalwares fuse with reused pieces to create unique, sometimes idiosyncratic rooms. Including pieces of tribal art adds to an atmosphere of eclectic style.

In these rooms, lighting can be used sparingly to create atmosphere or to spotlight important pieces, as well as to make a statement in itself. Plain walls and simple window treatments can create a subtle backdrop to a broad collection of contemporary designer pieces. However, adding pattern and color can also enhance the overall impression of the room. Pillows, throws, and rugs can be used to add contrasting textures and colors, too, as well as to bring together disparate elements to make a whole.

One benefit of a kitchen in a large, industrial space is that there is plenty of storage and work surface (*above right*). Here the space has been made more practical by including a circular trolley and a tiled freestanding unit that has pullout chopping boards to keep the food-preparation area compact.

White walls and stainless-steel cabinets contrast with a limed oak floor and re-purposed table and chairs in this kitchen (*right*).

Danny Lane's Luce Dei Miei Occhi 2 wall sculpture looks down on daily life in this living room. Orange-gold glass eyes and a stainless-steel wire frame create the outline of a face. The cut and polished poured glass is enhanced by sandblasted details.

Directory of designers and makers

Alvar Aalto (1898–1976), Finland
architect and furniture designer
Aalto started his own architecture practice in 1923, having studied at the University of Technology in Helsinki. In 1935, with his wife, Aino, he founded the furniture company Artek, which continues to produce his designs today. Aalto is best known for his designs for bent-plywood and laminated-wood furniture, including the cantilevered No. 31 chair he designed in 1930–31.

Eero Aarnio (b.1932), Finland
furniture and interior designer
Aarnio founded his own design office in 1962, five years after graduating from the Institute of Industrial Arts in Helsinki. His early work used craft techniques and natural materials, but in the 1960s he changed course and began to make space-age style fiberglass furniture, such as the Ball chair designed 1964–65.

Alessi design (founded 1921), Italy
metalware manufacturer
The Alessi firm started as a workshop and foundry, but has evolved to become a leader of Italian design. Since the 1970s it has worked with leading international designers such as Ettore Sottsass, Philippe Starck, Michael Graves, and the Campana Brothers to create innovative homewares.

Ron Arad (b.1951), Israel and U.K.
architect and designer
Arad studied at the Jerusalem Academy of Art and the Architectural Association in London. In 1981 he founded his own practice, One Off, with Caroline Thorman. He started Ron Arad Associates in 1989 and Ron Arad Architects in 2008. His innovative early pieces are considered to be "art" furniture; these include the 1981 Rover Chair. His later designs are more suited to mass production and are more sculptural in feel.

Ercole Barovier (1889–1974), Italy
glass designer
Barovier was born into a family of glassmakers who had worked on the Venetian island of Murano since the 14th century. He started his own workshop, Artisti Barovier (later Barovier e C.), on the island in 1919. There, he experimented with techniques and colored glass. In 1936 he took over the family business, Fratelli Barovier, and after 1947 worked with his son Angelo on vetro a fili—a series of striped glass vessels.

Harry Bertoia (1915–78), Italy and U.S.
sculptor and furniture designer
Bertoia arrived in the United States from Italy in 1930. He studied at the Detroit School of Arts and the Cranbrook Academy of Art, Michigan, where he took over the metal workshop in 1939. He later worked for Charles and Ray Eames and Hans and Florence Knoll. His designs for Knoll include the Diamond chair, part of a collection of five wire pieces he created in 1952. He later created sound sculptures.

Boch Frères (founded 1767), Belgium
ceramics factory
The factory was founded by Pierre-Joseph Boch (d.1818). In 1836 it merged and became known as Villeroy & Boch. In 1841, following the partitioning of Belgium and Luxembourg in 1839, the Belgian branch of the Boch family established a factory at Keramis that traded as Boch Frères. During the 1920s and 1930s it began producing the Art Deco pottery for which it is known today.

Edgar Brandt (1880–1960), France
metalworker
Brandt opened his business in Paris in 1902 and combined traditional forging methods with new technologies. He made wrought-iron pieces such as gates, radiator covers, and lamp bases and worked with glass manufacturer Daum Frères to create Art Nouveau chandeliers and lamps. After exhibiting at the 1925 Paris Exposition his work began to reflect the Art Deco style.

Marcel Breuer (1902–81), Hungary and U.S.
architect and furniture designer
After spending a short time studying fine art in Vienna, Breuer worked in an architect's office and then trained in carpentry at the Weimar Bauhaus (1920–23). While there he designed innovative tubular-steel and bent-plywood furniture, as well as numerous private houses and interiors. In 1937 he emigrated to the United States to teach at the Harvard School of Design.

José Zanine Caldas (1919–2011), Brazil
architect and furniture designer
In 1939 Caldas—a self-taught artist—set up a workshop in Rio to make scale models for architects such as Oscar Niemeyer. His first furniture designs date from the 1940s and were mass-produced from plywood under the name Móveis Artísticos Z. From the 1950s he made sculptural pieces chiseled from logs of native woods.

Fernando Campana (b.1961)
Humberto Campana (b.1953), Brazil
furniture designers
The Campana Brothers founded their company Estudio Campana in 1983. They were inspired by their native country to produce furniture using waste and recycled materials such as cardboard, rope, cloth, and scraps of wood. They came to international attention in 1989 with Gli inconfortabili (The Inconsolables), a furniture exhibition that concentrated on politics rather than functional objects. Pieces include the 1991 Favela chair that consists of glued and nailed wood off-cuts, and was inspired by Rio de Janeiro's shanty towns.

Wendell Castle (b.1932), U.S.
furniture designer
Castle studied sculpture and industrial design at the University of Kansas. In the 1960s, his experiments with fiberglass led to the creation of sculptural furniture, including the 1969 tooth-shaped Molar chair. A year later he started carving furniture from stack-laminated wood, turning his attention to solid wood in 1976. Castle is considered to be the father of the art furniture movement.

Demêtre Chiparus (1888–1950), Romania and France, *sculptor*
Chiparus worked in Paris from c.1914, where he created dramatic, elegant Art Deco figures, in cast bronze and carved ivory. He is renowned for female dancers depicted in elegant poses and exotic costumes that were inspired by the Ballets Russes and other dancers of the time. Other designs included theatrical, religious and sentimental sculptural subjects and ceramic busts and figures.

Clarice Cliff (1899–1972), U.K.
ceramic designer
In 1912 Cliff became an apprentice painter at the Lingard Webster Pottery in Tunstall, Staffordshire. Four years later she moved to A.J. Wilkinson, near Burslem, and in 1922 became an apprentice modeler. After visiting the Paris Exposition in 1925 her work was influenced by Art Deco and Cubism. She decorated discarded blank stock with bold patterns and colors to create her Bizarre series, which went on sale in 1928–29. Bizarre ware shapes followed, featuring triangular shapes and patterns outlined and filled with colored enamels.

Luigi Colani (b.1928), Germany
furniture designer
Colani's work is influenced by his education. He studied fine art in Berlin in 1946 and aerodynamics in Paris from 1948. He moved to America, where he worked for California aircraft manufacturer Douglas until 1954, when he returned to Europe. There he worked for firms such as Rosenthal and BMW. His ergonomically designed furniture includes the 1973 Korperform (body form) chair.

Joe Colombo (1930–71), Italy
architect and furniture designer
After training as a painter, and then as an architect, at the Polytechnic Institute of Milan, Colombo moved on to work as a designer in 1958. A year later he took over his father's electronics company and began to experiment with new techniques and materials. He opened his own design office in Milan in 1962. His designs included the 1970 Boby trolley.

Susie Cooper (1902–95), U.K.
ceramic designer
Cooper studied at Burslem School of Art and taught there, before working as a painter with A.E. Gray and Co. in 1922. She soon became the factory's resident designer, and in 1929 started Susie Cooper Pottery. The company initially bought blank white wares and hand-painted them with her patterns. A year later it moved to the Crown works in Burslem, where Wood & Sons supplied plain earthenware forms to Susie's own designs.

Lucienne Day (1917–2010), U.K.
textile designer
From 1934–37, Lucienne Conradi studied at Croydon School of Art. She then moved to the Royal College of Art, where she met her future husband, the furniture designer Robin Day. Her best-known design—Calyx—was commissioned for the 1952 Festival of Britain and won a gold medal at the 1951 Milan Triennale. She was presented with three awards by the Council of Industrial Design.

Tom Dixon (b.1959), Tunisia and U.K.
designer
Dixon dropped out of art school and began to design while recovering from a motorbike accident in 1983. He gained attention selling limited-edition welded furniture—such as his S and Pylon chairs—and then opened a shop—Space—to sell his work. He went on to be head of design at the Habitat retail chain and Artek, the Finnish furniture manufacturer, and creative director of 100% Design. He established his company, Tom Dixon, in 2002.

Christopher Dresser (1834–1904), U.K.
designer
Dresser studied botany at the new Government School of Design and is considered to be the first industrial designer. He promoted design reform, used modern manufacturing techniques, and designed wallpaper, textiles, ceramics, glass, furniture, and metalware. Nature influenced his early work, but Japanese, ancient Andean, and Egyptian forms and Classical antiquity also played a part. His designs were produced by the Linthorpe Art Pottery, Hukin and Heath, Richard Perry, Son & Co., James Dixon & Sons, and many others.

Charles Eames (1908–78)
Ray Eames (1912–88), U.S.
architect and furniture designers
Architect Charles Eames opened an office in 1930. He joined the faculty of the Cranbrook Academy of Art, Michigan, in 1939. There he met his future wife, weaving student Ray Kaiser. They moved to California, where they began to create ground-breaking furnishings from molded plywood and fiberglass. From 1949 their designs were produced by Herman Miller.

Piero Fornasetti (1913–88), Italy
furniture and interior designer
From 1930–32 Fornasetti studied at the Brera Academy of Fine Art in Milan. He went on to design glass for Venini, and posters and covers for the influential *Domus* and *Graphus* magazines. He started to work with Gio Ponti in 1940, creating interiors and furniture decorated with his surreal, signature Neo-classical motifs.

Pedro Friedeberg (b.1936), Italy and Mexico
furniture designer
Friedeberg began to study architecture, but did not complete his studies. Instead, he started to create surrealist artworks and furniture, such as the Hand-Chair, a sculpture/chair where the palm forms the seat and the fingers the back and armrests. He has a reputation for being an eccentric, and considers art to be dead because nothing new is being produced.

Simon Gate (1883–1945), Sweden
glass designer
Gate joined the Orrefors factory in 1916 and worked with master glassblower Knut Bergkvist to create a new technique called Graal, in which multiple layered cameo glass is cased with clear crystal. It was used to create decorative pieces such as vases, but Gate also designed tableware. He worked with the engraver Gustaf Abels to create a series of designs decorated with of nudes. His work was exhibited at the 1925 Paris Exposition.

Frank Gehry (b.1929), Canada and U.S.
architect and furniture designer
Gehry was born in Canada and moved to Los Angeles in 1947, where he studied at the City College and later graduated from the University of Southern California's School of Architecture. He is possibly best known for his architecture—*Vanity Fair* magazine labeled him "the most important architect of our age"—but he has also designed furniture, notably the Easy Edges series 1969–73.

Michael Graves (1934–2015), U.S.
architect and designer
Graves studied architecture at the University of Cincinnati and Harvard, then spent two years at the American Academy in Rome. He set up his own practice in 1964 and went on to be one of the founders of the Post Modern style, taking motifs from classical architecture and using them in a witty way. He also designed homewares, including the 1985 Whistling Bird kettle for Alessi, which has become the company's best-seller, with more than 2 million sold at the time of his death.

Hagenauer (1898–1986), Austria
metalworking factory
The Hagenauer workshop was founded by gold- and silversmith Carl Hagenauer and began by making Art Nouveau pieces. His son Karl joined in 1919 and his designs include simple tea and coffee services. Carl's youngest son, Franz, joined in 1925. He was a member of the Wiener Werkstätte and studied at the College of Applied Arts in Vienna. He designed brass sculptures influenced by the Art Deco fascination with African art. During the 1950s the company made some wooden sculptures.

Edward Hald (1883–1980), Sweden
glass designer
Hald—a painter who had trained with Henri Matisse—joined the Swedish glassworks Orrefors in 1917. With Simon Gate he was employed to update and improve the company's designs. In the 1930s he developed a variation of the Graal technique, known as Fishgraal. A design is painted onto glass with liquid bitumen. The layer that isn't the patterned is acid-etched away, so that the pattern stands out on a clear background. It is then cased in clear glass.

Josef Hoffmann (1870–1956), Austria
architect and designer
Hoffmann studied at the Academy of Fine Art in Vienna, graduating with a Prix de Rome in 1895. With Koloman Moser he helped to found the Vienna Secession in 1897; in 1903 he founded the Wiener Werkstätte. Hoffmann designed furniture (many pieces were produced by Thonet), metalwork, glass (designs were made for J.&L. Lobmeyer) and jewellery. Although often identified as an Art Nouveau designer, his geometric style is closer to the work of Charles Rennie Mackintosh.

Arne Jacobsen (1902–71), Denmark
designer and architect
Jacobsen began his career by studying to be a mason, before attending the Royal Danish Academy of Fine Art in Copenhagen, graduating in 1927. He made his name designing sculptural chairs such as the 1955 Series 7 and 1957–58 Swan and Egg. He also designed metalware for Stelton and Michelsen, lighting for Louis Poulsen and architectural projects, including the Radisson SAS Hotel, Copenhagen.

Georg Jensen (1866–1935), Denmark
silversmith
Jensen trained as a goldsmith as an apprentice in Copenhagen and as a sculptor at the Royal Academy of Fine Arts in the city. He worked as a potter before returning to silversmithing in 1901, working for another silversmith before setting up his own workshop in 1904. He made Art Nouveau-style pieces that, by the 1920s, were being sold in Jensen's own stores in New York, London, Paris, Stockholm, and Berlin. He employed many designers, including Johan Rohde and Henning Koppel. The company continues today.

Finn Juhl (1912–89), Denmark
furniture designer
Juhl graduated from the Royal Danish Academy of Fine Art in Copenhagen in 1934 after studying architecture. He went on to design furniture with Niels Vodder before opening his own office in 1945. He helped to popularize the use of teak in Danish design and designed sculptural, well-crafted furniture such as the 1949 Chieftains chair.

Vladimir Kagan (b.1927), Germany and U.S.
furniture designer
Kagan emigrated to the United States in 1938. He studied architecture at Columbia University and in 1947 began to work with his cabinetmaker father, Illi Kagan. Two years later he opened a shop in New York, where his sculptural, curvaceous, and organic furniture was bought by clients ranging from General Motors to Marilyn Monroe.

Poul Kjærholm (1929–80), Denmark
furniture designer
Kjærholm trained as a carpenter and then studied furniture design and cabinetmaking at the Copenhagen School of Arts and Crafts. His elegant furniture combined natural materials and metal, and was designed to be mass-produced. Pieces such as the PK22 chair were first manufactured by E. Kold Christensen, and later by Fritz Hansen. Kjærholm taught at the Royal Danish Academy of Fine Art in Copenhagen for over 20 years.

Florence Knoll (b.1917), U.S.
furniture designer
Architecture student Florence Schust studied at the Cranbrook Academy of Art, Michigan, and the Architectural Association in London. In 1943 she joined Hans Knoll's furniture company, marrying him and becoming his business partner in 1946. That year they formed Knoll Associates, and Florence pioneered the popular modern Knoll look and the company's innovative approach to room-planning.

Shiro Kuramata (1934–91), Japan
furniture designer
Kuramata studied architecture at Tokyo Polytechnic and interior design at the Kuwazawa Institute for Design in Tokyo as well as working for the Japanese furniture manufacturer Teikokukizai and the Tokyo department store Matsuya. He began his own design practice in 1965 and created interiors and furniture. Notable designs include the 1986 How High the Moon chair, made from nickel-plated metal, which has a light and airy transparency. He worked with the Memphis group in the 1980s.

René Lalique (1860–1945), France
jeweler and glass designer
Lalique studied drawing and graphic design in Paris and London before starting to design jewelry for firms such as Cartier. He opened his own jewelry business in Paris 1885, making intricate Art Nouveau pieces. He began to experiment with glass in the mid-1890s, and went on to turn an industrial process into an art form. Lalique used his knowledge of the chemistry of glass to develop opalescent glass in a range of colors. At the Paris Exposition of 1925 he received acclaim for his Art Deco glassware.

Danny Lane (b.1955), U.S. and U.K.
sculptor and furniture designer
Lane trained as a painter , before going on to explore two- and three-dimensional forms. His sculpture and furniture ranges from domestic pieces to Borealis at the GM Renaissance Center, Detroit, one of the world's largest glass sculptures. He uses stacked and fractured glass and twisted or rusted steel in his work. With Ron Arad and Tom Dixon, he was part of the avant-garde furniture movement of the 1980s, thanks to pieces such as his 1986 sculptural glass Etruscan Chair.

Le Corbusier (1887–1965), Switzerland and France, *architect and furniture designer*
Born Charles-Édouard Jeanneret, Le Corbusier built his first house in his native Switzerland when he was 18 and adopted his pseudonym in c.1920. In 1922 he set up an architectural practice with his cousin Pierre Jeanneret in Paris. Five years later the two men, with Charlotte Perriand, began designing the functional tubular-steel furniture that has come to epitomize the International Style.

Vicke Lindstrand (1904–83), Sweden
glass and ceramic designer
Lindstrand began as a student of graphic design at the Swedish Arts and Crafts Association School in Gothenburg. From 1928–41 he produced glass designs for Orrefors as well as pieces for the Karlskrona porcelain factory and Uppsala-Ekeby ceramics factory. He became art director of Uppsala-Ekeby in 1943. From 1950 he ran his own design studio and worked as design director for glass factory Kosta Boda.

Josef Lorenzl (1892–1950), Austria
sculptor and ceramic designer
Lorenzl trained at the Vienna Arsenal foundry and went on to design bronze and chryselephantine figures for the company. His most desirable pieces feature female dancers depicted in elegant, athletic poses and often wearing revealing garments. He also designed ceramic figures for Goldscheider. These show a similar appreciation for the female form.

Ingeborg Lundin (1921–92), Denmark
glass designer
Lundin became Orrefors' first female designer when she joined the company in 1947. She went on to design the Apple vase, which has come to be regarded as one of the best-known pieces of 1950s glass. She is also known for the glass she decorated using the engraved Graal technique.

Per Lütken (1916–98), Denmark
glass designer
Lütken studied painting at the School of Arts and Crafts in Copenhagen. He joined Holmegaard in 1942 and created a wide range of designs for them, including mass-produced tablewares and one-off glass sculptures. He was also responsible for designing the majority of Holmegaard's marketing material.

Charles Rennie Mackintosh (1868–1928), Scotland, *architect and designer*
Mackintosh worked in the architecture practice of Honeyman and Keppie in Glasgow, from 1889 to 1914, becoming a partner in 1901. He became a leading exponent of the Glasgow School style, which aimed to innovate, rather than replicate historical styles. He is best known for his designs for Glasgow School of Art and Hill House in Helensburgh. The first of his high-backed chairs with distinctive oval top rail was designed for the interior of Miss Kate Cranston's Argyle Street tearoom.

Dino Martens (1894–1970), Italy
glass designer
Martens was a student at the Academy of Fine Art in Venice where he concentrated on painting. During the 1920s and 1930s he worked as a painter for a number of Muranese glassworks. In 1939 he took over the role of artistic director at Aureliano Toso. He worked there until 1965, designing influential glass including the Oriente and Zanfirico ranges.

Jean Mayodon (1893–1967), France
ceramic designer
Mayodon designed large-scale ceramics for interiors as well as domestic decorative wares. His vases, bowls and plates are usually subdued in shape, but many were decorated in a Classical style with mythological sea creatures and female nudes in the geometric and stylized form popular in the Art Deco period. Others depicted modern subjects, such as the dancer Isadora Duncan. He was made artistic director of the Sèvres porcelain factory in 1934 and became its director in 1941.

Alessandro Mendini (b.1931), Italy
designer and architect
Mendini studied architecture at the Polytechnic Institute in Milan, graduating in 1959. He worked as a designer with Marcello Nizzoli. In 1979 he became a member of Studio Alchimia, a forerunner of the Memphis group and Post Modern design. His designs—such as the 1978 Proust armchair—mix forms from different cultures and eras.

Ludwig Mies van der Rohe (1886–1969), Germany and U.S.
architect and furniture designer
Mies van der Rohe was apprenticed to the Modernist architect Peter Behrens and opened his own office in Berlin in 1912. His first tubular-metal chair—the MR10—was designed with Lily Reich in 1927. His Barcelona chair, also designed with Reich, was originally designed for the German Pavilion at the 1929 Barcelona International Exposition. He was appointed director of the Bauhaus in 1930 but left in 1933. He moved to the U.S. in 1937, where he worked as an architect.

Carlo Mollino (1905–73), Italy
furniture designer
Mollino graduated from the School of Architecture in Turin in 1931, having previously studied engineering and art history. His furniture is usually biomorphic in shape, reflecting his interest in Futurism and Surrealism, and was often designed for specific buildings. His characteristic exuberant style is often referred to as "Turinese Baroque."

Forrest Myers (b.1941), U.S.
sculptor and furniture designer
Myers studied at the San Francisco Art Institute, graduating in 1960. He moved to New York a year later and in the early to mid-1960s was a founding member of the Park Place Gallery. His sculptural furniture is made from twisted aluminium coil. His most famous work is *The Wall* (1973), a monumental wall sculpture in SoHo, New York.

George Nelson (1907–86), U.S.
furniture designer
Nelson left Yale in 1931 after studying art and architecture. He then attended the American Academy in Rome. He is credited with having introduced Americans to European Modernism through the articles he wrote for *Pencil Points* and *Architectural Form* after 1935. From 1946 to 1972 he was director of design at Herman Miller, where he worked with Charles Eames and Isamu Noguchi.

Marc Newson (b.1963), Australia and U.K.
designer
Newson studied jewellery and sculpture at the Sydney College of the Arts and graduated in 1984. Two years later his first exhibition included one of his best-known designs, the Lockheed Lounge. He moved to Tokyo, before setting up a studio in Paris in 1991, and a subsequent move to London. He described his 1988 Embryo Chair as "one of the first pieces where I hit upon a discernible style." Newson works across a wide range of disciplines, from furniture and household objects to aircraft and yachts.

Isamu Noguchi (1904–88), U.S.
sculptor and designer
Noguchi was born in Los Angeles, but spent some of his childhood in Japan. In the early 1920s he quit medical school to study sculpture in New York and worked in Paris as an assistant to the sculptor Constantin Brancusi for two years from 1927. He returned to the U.S. in 1932, where he worked as a sculptor, but also designed paper lamps, furniture for Herman Miller and Knoll, and glassware for Steuben.

Verner Panton (1926–98), Denmark
designer
Panton studied architecture at the Royal Danish Academy of Fine Art in Copenhagen, graduating in 1951. He went on to work for Arne Jacobsen (from 1952–55), before setting up his own design studio in 1955. He designed furniture, lighting, carpets, and other textiles in a bold, innovative, and playful style.

Gaetano Pesce (b.1939), Italy
furniture designer
Pesce studied architecture and industrial design at the Ca' Foscari University of Venice. After graduating in 1965 he went to work for companies such as Cassina, Venini and C&B Italia using new materials and techniques to create innovative pieces that reflect his sense of humour. These include the 1969 anthropomorphic U series of chairs and sofas.

Warren Platner (1919–2006), U.S.
furniture designer
Platner graduated from Cornell University in 1941 having studied architecture. He worked for Raymond Loewy and I. M. Pei from 1945 until 1950, and then Eero Saarinen from 1960 until 1965. Platner is best known for the wire-framed furniture he designed for Knoll in 1966.

Flavio Poli (1900–84), Italy
glass designer
Poli studied ceramics, but in 1929 joined I.V.A.M. on Murano as a glass sculptor. Five years later he joined the Seguso-Barovier-Ferro glass factory, and he was promoted to artistic director in 1963. His best-known pieces are the colorful cased-glass vases he designed in the 1950s.

Gio Ponti (1891–1979), Italy
designer
In 1921 Ponti graduated in architecture from the Polytechnic Institute in Milan. Seven years later he launched the influential design journal *Domus* and he went on to design buildings, furniture, glass, ceramics and metalware. His best-known pieces include the Superleggera chair, designed for Cassina in 1957, furniture designed with Piero Fornasetti, and ceramics he created for Richard Ginori.

Ferdinand Preiss (1882–1943), Germany
sculptor
In 1897 Preiss was apprenticed to the ivory carver Philipp Willmann. In 1906, with Arthur Kassler, he founded Preiss-Kassler, which was based in Berlin and produced chryselephantine figures in the Classical style. During the 1920s and 1930s, Preiss-Kassler produced bronze and ivory figures on marble bases in the Art Deco style. These usually feature athletic young women in graceful, elegant poses.

Karim Rashid (b.1960), Egypt and U.S.
designer
Rashid was born in Cairo and raised in Canada. He studied industrial design at Carleton University in Ottawa, Canada, and graduated in 1982. Since then he has designed more than 3,000 objects, including furniture, packaging and lighting. His work can be identified by its sensual curves and bright colors and includes the Oh chair for Umbra, watches and tableware for Alessi, and lighting for Artemide.

Sergio Rodrigues (1927–2014), Brazil
architect and furniture designer
Rodrigues graduated from the National School of Architecture in Rio de Janeiro in 1952. He ran a furniture and modern art store before founding his own furniture company, Oca, in 1955. In 1968 he left Oca to work as an independent designer. His work usually features local, natural materials such as rattan, leather, and wood. His 1957 Sheriff chair is probably his best-known piece.

Emile-Jacques Ruhlmann (1879–1933), France
furniture designer
Ruhlmann took over his father's painting and contracting firm after his father's death in 1907. He exhibited his first designs—including furniture, fabric and lamps—at the Salon d'Automne in Paris in 1913. The firm merged with Pierre Laurent in 1919 to become Ruhlmann & Laurent. Ruhlmann opened his own cabinetmaking company, employing the finest craftsmen and draughtsmen, in 1923. He is known for using rich, exotic woods and other materials to create modern, clean and sophisticated, exquisitely crafted furnishings.

Eero Saarinen (1910–61), Finland and U.S.
architect and furniture designer
Saarinen, the son of architect Eliel Saarinen, moved from Finland to the U.S. with his family in 1923. From 1929 to 1930 he studied sculpture in Paris, and then architecture at Yale. In 1937, three years after graduating, he worked with Charles Eames. Their moulded plywood-shell armchair won the Organic Design in Home Furnishings award in 1940. He then began to design organically shaped furniture for Knoll, including the 1948 Womb chair.

Ettore Sottsass (1917–2007), Austria and Italy
architect and furniture designer
Sottsass studied architecture in Turin, graduating in 1939. In 1946 he moved to Milan and for the next decade he worked as a curator, writer and designer and set up an architecture and industrial design practice. He became artistic director of Poltronova in 1957 and design consultant for Olivetti in 1958, but is best-known for his work with the Memphis group, which he co-founded in 1981. His work for Memphis includes designs for furniture, glass, ceramics and jewelry.

Philippe Starck (b.1949), France
designer
After studying at the École Camondo in Paris, Starck set up his first company, which produced inflatable objects, in 1968. During the 1970s he created interiors, such as that of the Paris nightclub La Main Bleue. Other notable interiors include the private apartments in the Élysée Palace (1983–84) in Paris and the Royalton and Paramount hotels (1988 and 1990) in New York City. Furnishings from these interiors have been produced for domestic settings. Starck has also designed a wide range of objects, including the Juicy Salif juicer for Alessi and office furniture for Vitra.

Steuben (1903–2011), U.S.
glassworks
Under the directorship of English glassmaker and chemist Frederick Carder, the company, based in Corning, Steuben County, New York, produced a range of artistic glassware including the iridescent Aurene (introduced 1904). In 1932, the company developed a pure, colorless crystal glass that was ideal for acid etching, cutting, and engraving. Known as 10M, it soon dominated production, and colored glass was discontinued in 1933. The company closed in 2011, but from 2014 a limited range of designs was produced for the Corning Museum of Glass.

Gebruder Thonet (founded 1819), Austria
furniture makers
Michael Thonet set up a cabinetmaking business, specializing in parquetry, in 1819. He began experimenting with bentwood and by the 1930s had devised a revolutionary process to boil or steam lengths of beechwood in water and then bend them to form long curved rods for chair frames. The result was an inexpensive yet durable chair that eliminated the need for hand-carved joints. He perfected the mechanized process in 1859. The firm continues in business today.

Ermanno Toso (1903–73), Italy
glass designer
Toso joined Fratelli Toso, the Murano glassmaking factory set up by his grandfather and five of his brothers, in 1924. In 1936 he was promoted to marketing and artistic director. Toso introduced a new Modern style to the company's output. Many of the pieces he designed used updated versions of traditional techniques such as murrines.

Paolo Venini (1895–1959), Italy
glass designer
Venini trained as a lawyer but set up a glassworks with Giacomo Cappellin in 1921. He set up his own factory four years later and developed innovative new forms of glass, such as vetro pulegoso (bubbled glass). The company produced many famous designs by key designers in the 1950s and 1960s.

Hans Wegner (1914–2007), Denmark
furniture designer
Wegner worked as an apprentice carpenter before studying at the Copenhagen Institute of Technology (1936–38) and later at the School of Arts and Crafts in the city. He worked with Arne Jacobsen and Erik Møller from 1940 and set up his own studio in 1946. His best-known pieces are made from solid wood—often teak—and were produced by companies including Fritz Hansen.

WMF (founded 1853), Germany
metalware factory
The original factory was founded in Geislingen by Daniel Straub. It amalgamated with several firms and in 1880 became known as WMF—the Württembergische Metallwarenfabrik. Although it is best known for its Art Nouveau metalware, particularly designs with a maiden motif, it introduced Art Deco styles in the 1920s. These included the Ikora metalware pieces and a range of glass that included the iridescent Myra and the heavier Ikora glass, which was decorated with colors and bubbles.

Frank Lloyd Wright (1867–1959), U.S.
architect and designer
Wright studied architecture and engineering before working in the Chicago practice of Louis Sullivan, where he designed homes for Adler & Sullivan. He opened his own practice in Chicago in 1893, where he developed the Prairie School style. The homes he designed were influenced by the surrounding prairie and his appreciation of Japanese design. His reputation as a furniture designer is based on the pieces he designed for these buildings.

Suppliers and sources

FLEA MARKETS

Aachener Platz Flea & Antique Market
Dusseldorf, Germany
Every Saturday morning

Albertbrücke Flea Market
Dresden, Germany
Every Saturday and Sunday

Alte Leipziger Messe
Leipzig, Germany
First Sunday of the month between March and November

Altstadt-Flohmarkt am Hohen Ufer
Hanover, Germany
Every Saturday

Arezzo Flea Market
Arezzo, Italy
First Saturday and Sunday of every month

Arkonaplatz Flea Market
Berlin, Germany
Every Sunday

Birkelunden Flea Market
Oslo, Norway
Every Saturday

Braderie de Lille Flea Market
France
Annual two-day event in September

Brocante Château Cheval
Waterloo, Belgium
Every Sunday morning

Bürgerweide Flea Market
Bremen, Germany
Every Sunday

Carmagnoia Flea Market
Turin, Italy
Every second Sunday of the month
(except August)

Ciney Expo Flea Market
Ciney, Belgium
Annual 4-day event in March

Place du Jeu de Balle Flea Market
Brussels, Belgium
Every day

**Porte de Clignancourt Flea Markets
(Les Puces de Saint-Ouen)**
Paris, France
Weekends

Porte de Vanves
Paris, France
Weekends

Cormano Flea Market
Cormano, Italy
Saturdays 7.30am–2pm

El Rastro Flea Markets
Madrid, Spain
Every Sunday and public holiday

Flohschanze Flea Market in Schanzenviertel
Hamburg, Germany
Every Saturday and Sunday

Kavalleriemarkt
Munich, Germany
Every Friday and Saturday

Lake Maggiore Flea Market
Borgo D'Ale, Italy
Every third Sunday of the month

Mauerpark Flea Market
Berlin, Germany
Every Sunday

Mirepoix Flea Market
Auriac-sur-Vendinelle, France
One weekend in May

Münchner Flohmarkt auf der Theresienwiese
Munich, Germany
Once a year on the first Saturday of Munich's Spring Festival (in April)

Portobello Road Flea Market
London, U.K.
Every Saturday, although there are stalls from Monday to Friday

Vrijmarkt Amsterdam Flea Market
Amsterdam, Natherlands
One Saturday in April

ANTIQUES MARKETS & FAIRS

Alfies Antique Market
London, U.K.
www.alfiesantiques.com

Brimfield Antique Show
Massachusetts, U.S.
www.brimfield.com
5,000 dealers from all over the country

Cynthia Findlay
Toronto Antiques on King
www.torontoantiquesonking.com

Grays Antiques Market
London, U.K.
www.graysantiques.com

Round Top
Texas, U.S.
www.roundtoptexasantiques.com

AUCTION HOUSES

Bellmans
www.bellmans.co.uk

Cheffins
www.cheffins.co.uk

Clevedon Salerooms
www.clevedon-salerooms.com

Dorotheum
www.dorotheum.com

Dreweatts and Bloomsbury
www.dreweatts.com

Duke's
www.dukes-auctions.com

Dunbar Sloane
www.dunbarsloane.co.nz

Fielding's
www.fieldingsauctioneers.co.uk

Auktionhaus Dr Fischer
www.auctions-fischer.de

Freeman's
www.freemansauction.com

Gardiner Houlgate
www.gardinerhoulgate.co.uk

Gorringes
www.gorringes.co.uk

Hampton and Littlewood
www.hamptonandlittlewood.co.uk

Hartleys
www.andrewhartleyfinearts.co.uk

Leslie Hindman Auctioneers
www.lesliehindman.com

Im Kinsky
www.imkinsky.com

James D Julia Inc.
www.juliaauctions.com

Lawrences' Auctioneers
www.lawrences.co.uk

Lyon and Turnbull Ltd
www.lyonandturnbull.com

Michaan's
www.michaans.com

Pook & Pook
www.pookandpook.com

Quittenbaum
www.quittenbaum.de

Rago Arts and Auction Center
www.ragoarts.com

Skinner Inc.
www.skinnerinc.com

Sotheby's
www.sothebys.com

Swann Galleries
www.swanngalleries.com

Sworders
www.sworder.co.uk

Kerry Taylor Auctions
www.kerrytaylorauctions.com

Tennants
www.tennants.co.uk

Von Zezschwitz
www.von-zezschwitz.de

Woolley and Wallis
www.woolleyandwallis.co.uk

Richard Wright
www.wright20.com

DEALERS

Calderwood Gallery
www.calderwoodgallery.com

Glass etc.
www.decanterman.com

Jeanette Hayhurst Fine Glass
www.antiqueglass-london.com

Hickmet Fine Arts
www.hickmetfineart.com

Mark Hill
www.markhill.net

Macklowe Gallery
www.macklowegallery.com

Francesca Martire, Alfies Antiques Market
www.francescamartire.com

Mike and Debby Moir Glass
www.manddmoir.co.uk

Lillian Nassau
www.lilliannassau.com

R & Company
www.r-and-company.com

Geoffrey Robinson, Alfies Antiques Market
www.robinsonantiques.co.uk

Van Den Bosch
www.vandenbosch.com

SUPPLIERS OF NEW FURNITURE

Herman Miller
www.hermanmiller.com

Knoll
www.knoll.com

Vitra
www.vitra.com

MUSEUMS

Alvar Aalto Museum
Jyväskylä, Finland
www.alvaraalto.fi

Bauhaus Archive
Berlin, Germany
www.bauhaus.de

Chicago Atheneam Museum of Architecture and Design
U.S.
www.chi-athenaeum.org

Cooper Hewitt National Design Museum
New York, U.S.
www.cooperhewitt.org

Design Museum
Helsinki, Finland
www.designmuseum.fi

Design Museum
London, U.K.
www.designmuseum.org

Designmuseum
Copenhagen, Denmark
www.designmuseum.dk

Geffrye Museum
London, U.K.
www.geffrye-museum.org.uk

The Metropolitan Museum of Art
New York, U.S.
www.metmuseum.org

Musée des Arts Décoratifs
Paris, France
www.lesartsdecoratifs.fr

The Museum of Modern Art
New York, U.S.
www.moma.org

Die Neue Sammlung
Munich, Germany
www.die-neue-sammlung.de

Victoria and Albert Museum
London, U.K.
www.vam.ac.uk

Vitra Design Museum
Weil am Rhein, Germany
www.design-museum.de

Index

Figures in *italics* indicate captions

Acknowledgments

The publishers would like to thank the following organizations for supplying pictures for use in this book:

Bellmans
New Pound, Wisborough Green
Billingshurst, West Sussex, U.K.
Tel: +44 1403 700858
www.bellmans.co.uk
page **269** top

Calderwood Gallery
1622 Spruce Street
Philadelphia PA 19123, U.S.
Tel: +1 215 546 5357
www.calderwoodgallery.com
page **38** left, page **38** right, page **39** bottom right

Dorotheum
Palais Dorotheum
Dorotheergasse 17
A-1010 Vienna, Austria
Tel: +43 1 515 600
www.dorotheum.com
page **20** left, page **20** center, page **51** top left, page **51** center left, page **51** center right, page **122** right, page **127** bottom left, page **168** center, page **168** bottom, page **181** top right, page **181** bottom right, page **199** top right, page **206** bottom

Dreweatts and Bloomsbury
Donnington Priory, Newbury
Berkshire RG14 2JE, U.K.
Tel: +44 163 555 3553
www.dreweatts.com
page **206** top right

Duke's
The Dorchester Fine Art Saleroom
Weymouth Avenue
Dorchester, Dorset DT1 1QS, U.K.
+44 1305 265080
www.dukes-auctions.com
page **122** bottom left

Fielding's
Mill Race Lane, Stourbridge
West Midlands, DY8 1JN, U.K.
Tel: +1384 444140
www.fieldingsauctioneers.co.uk
page **35** top left, page **35** top right, page **35** bottom left, page **200** top

Auktionhaus Dr Fischer
Trappensee-Schößchen
D-74074 Heilbronn, Germany
Tel: +49 7131155570
www.auctions-fischer.de
page **181** center, page **181** center right

Freeman's
1808 Chestnut Street
Philadelphia PA 19103, U.S.
Tel: +1 215 563 9275
www.freemansauction.com
page **108** bottom, page **175** bottom left

Gorringes
15 North Street
Lewes, East Sussex BN7 2PD, U.K.
Tel: +44 127 347 2503
www.gorringes.co.uk
page **35** bottom right

Hickmet Fine Arts
85 Portobello Road
London W11 2QB
+44 207 243 6365, U.K.
www.hickmetfineart.com
page **30** top, page **43**

Leslie Hindman Auctioneers
1338 West Lake Street
Chicago IL 60607, U.S.
Tel: +1 312 280 1212
www.lesliehindman.com
page **175** center

Im Kinsky
Palais Kinsky Freyung 4
A-1010 Vienna, Austria
Tel: +43 1 532 42 009
www.imkinsky.com
page **19** right, page **45** bottom right, page **95** top right, page **106** center, page **198** bottom

Lyon and Turnbull Ltd
33 Broughton Place
Edinburgh EH1 3RR, U.K.
Tel: +44 131 557 8844
www.lyonandturnbull.com
page **17** center, page **18** right, page **22** top, page **49**, page **95** top left, page **135** bottom, page **197** bottom, page **199** top left, page **207** top left, page **207** bottom left

Lillian Nassau
220 East 57th Street
New York NY 10022, U.S.
Tel: +1 212 759-6062
www.lilliannassau.com
page **62** bottom

Quittenbaum
Theresienstrasse 60
D-80333 Munich , Germany
Tel: +49 89 2737021-25
www.quittenbaum.de
page **16** left, page **19** left, page **21** right, page **22** bottom, page **23** left, page **24**, page **25** center, page **29** right, page **40** center, page **44**, page **45**, page **46** top left, page **46** top right, page **46** bottom right, page **48**, page **68** bottom left, page **69** top right, page **69** bottom, page **71** bottom right, page **121** bottom left, page **164**, page **175** top left, page **175** top right, page **175** bottom right, page **175** bottom center, page **178** top, page **194** bottom, page **195** top, page **196**, page **203** top left, page **203** top right, page **203** bottom right, page **206** top left, page **207** center, page **215**, page **226**, page **234**, page **248** bottom right, page **249** center, page **265** bottom left, page **268** bottom

R & Company
82 Franklin Street
New York NY 10013, U.S.
+1 212 343 7979
www.r-and-company.com
page **115**, page **119**, page **124**, page **200** center left, page **200** bottom

Rago Arts and Auction Center
333 North Main Street
Lambertville NJ 08530, U.S.
Tel: +1 609 397 9374
www.ragoarts.com
page **16** right, page **17** right, page **18** left, page **21** left, page **23** right, page **25** left, page **25** right, page **36** top, page **36** bottom, page **39** bottom left, page **39** bottom right, page **47** bottom right, page **65** bottom, page **68** top, page **68** bottom right, page **71** bottom left, page **74**, page **96** bottom, page **97** top, page **98**, page **105**, page **106** left, page **115** bottom right, page **116**, page **119** center, page **121**, page **125**, page **127** center left, page **127** center right, page **130**, page **135**, page **136** top, page **137** top, page **137** bottom, page **159**, page **167**, page **168** top left, page **169**, page **172**, page **178** bottom right, page **182** top right, page **132**, page **133**, page **194** top, page **195** bottom left, page **198** top, page **199** bottom, page **200** center right, page **203** bottom left, page **216**, page **224**, page **226** top, page **229**, page **231** center, page **231** bottom, page **232**, page **244**, page **247** top, page **250**, page **262** bottom, page **268** top left, page **269** bottom, page **270**

Skinner Inc.
The Heritage on the Garden
63 Park Plaza
Boston MA 02116, U.S.
Tel: +1 617 350 5400
www.skinnerinc.com
page **109**, page **137** center, page **247** bottom

Sotheby's
34–35 New Bond Street
London W1A 2AA, U.K.
www.sothebys.com
page **28** bottom, page **72** top, page **230** center, page **248** bottom left, page **249** bottom

Swann Galleries
104 East 25th Street
New York, NY 10010 , U.S.
Tel: +1 212 254 4710
www.swanngalleries.com
page **31**, page **32** bottom, page **34**

Sworders
14 Cambridge Road
Stansted Mountfitchet
Essex CM24 8BZ, U.K.
Tel: +44 127 981 7778
www.sworder.co.uk
page **47** top

Tennants
The Auction Center
Leyburn, North Yorkshire
DL8 5SG, U.K.
Tel: +44 1969 623780
www.tennants.co.uk
page **204**

Von Zezschwitz
Friedrichstrasse 1a
80801 Munich, Germany
+49 89 38 98 930
www.von-zezschwitz.de
page **17** left, page **40** left, page **40** right, page **51** left, page **51** top center, page **51** top right, page **181** bottom left, page **207** top right

Woolley and Wallis
51–61 Castle Street
Salisbury, Wiltshire SP1 3SU, U.K.
Tel: +44 172 242 4500
www.woolleyandwallis.co.uk
page **90** bottom, page **96** top, page **123** left, page **182** top left, page **199** top center, page **231** top left

Artists'/Designers' copyright:

page **17** far left Richard Riemerschmid © DACS 2015 / page **19** left Henry van de Velde © DACS 2015 / page **32** center right Jean Cocteau © ADAGP, Paris and DACS, London 2015 / page **33** Duncan Grant © Estate of Duncan Grant. All rights reserved, DACS 2015 / page **52** top Jacques Adnet © ADAGP, Paris and DACS, London 2015 /page **52** bottom Constantin Brancusi © ADAGP, Paris and DACS, London 2015 / page **66** below left Marianne Brandt © DACS 2015 / page **66** below right Charlotte Perriand & Pierre Jeanneret © ADAGP, Paris and DACS, London 2015 / page **74** Gerrit Rietveld © DACS 2015 / page **123** far right Axel Salto © DACS 2015 / page **125** top Stig Lindberg © Stig Lindberg / DACS 2015 / page **125** second from top Ingeborg Lundin © DACS 2015 / page **142** top Candida Höfer © Candida Höfer / VG Bild-Kunst, Bonn and DACS, London 2015 / page **142** top Jean Prouvé © ADAGP, Paris and DACS, London 2015 / page **181** top right Fulvio Bianconi © DACS 2015 / page **201** Andy Warhol © 2015 The Andy Warhol Foundation for the Visual Arts, Inc. / Artists Rights Society (ARS), New York and DACS, London / page **225** bottom right Javier Mariscal © DACS 2015 / page **227** Peter Franck © DACS 2015 / page **247** bottom Alexander Calder © 2015 Calder Foundation, New York / DACS London / page **269** bottom Arman © ADAGP, Paris and DACS, London 2015

Every effort has been made to trace the copyright holders and to provide accurate information. If there are omissions or inaccuracies please inform the Publisher so all necessary corrections can be made.